DEDICATION

First, I want to thank Jesus for being my Lord, Savior, and Life. Without Him, I can do nothing (John 15:5)! I also want to thank my wife, Carrie. She is everything to me. Unfortunately, she and my children had to watch me live through my false identity. I am so grateful that you never gave up on me. Holy Spirit definitely used you to "sand down" my rough edges. I love doing life with you, and you still make my heart beat fast. Thank you for cheering me on and supporting me through this writing process. Brycen, Regan, Corbin, Hudson, and Tyson, thank you for your forgiveness. You are fierce warriors, and I am so proud of each of you. I am very grateful to God to be your dad. I could not ask for better children. You guys are *the best!* Never forget, "Armor On, Shields Up, and Keep Moving." Thank you, Dad and Mom (Larry and Diane McKeehan), for being cheerleaders for my entire life. God knew what kind of parents I needed, and I believe He gave me the best! To my sister, Rachel, I love you, and the cup is mine. I am also grateful to have such amazing in-laws. Bill and Jackie, you have loved and supported me since I became a part of the family. Thank you!

I am so honored to work for Grace Fellowship International. Every day, I get to do something I love. I also get to do it with people I love and admire. Kristy, thank you for getting things done almost before I ask for it. Your passion for GFI and our vision both encourages and inspires me. John Norman, thank you for making me laugh and for sharing all of Dr. Solomon's "one-liners." You stepped in to help GFI, and we have never been the same. Dr. John Woodward, I will never be able to put into words all the ways you encourage and support me. You are a giant, and I am blessed to work alongside you. You teach me something new every day. Without you, this book would not be in print.

I am dedicating this book to three great men! Dr. Solomon, even though my time with you was brief, it was no doubt powerful! It is my desire to continue the legacy you left. I'm not sure we will ever truly know the impact you made, but there are thousands of lives living today in victory because of you. Blaine Anderson was a spiritual father to me. Years ago, I came to Chilhowee Hills Baptist Church with experiences of Holy Spirit but not a lot of knowledge. You helped me both to learn and grow. I can counsel and coach others because of the knowledge you imparted to me. You are with our Father in Heaven, and I miss you so much! Finally, Hans Haun, my mentor. Tears well up in my eyes as I can never thank you enough for teaching me the "Exchanged Life." I look forward to our weekly meetings, even now. Thank you for being a friend but also for pushing me to be better! You are no doubt one of the biggest reasons this book exists!

UNDERSTANDING YOUR IDENTITY
IN CHRIST

WHO DO YOU THINK YOU ARE?

MARK MCKEEHAN

Copyright © 2024 by Mark McKeehan

No part of this book may be used or reproduced in any manner whatsoever without written permission, except in the case of brief quotations embodied in critical articles and reviews.

ISBN: 978-1-963542-02-8

Published by:
Grace Fellowship International
PO Box 368
Pigeon Forge, TN 37868

www.GraceFellowshipInternational.com
Mark@gracefellowshipinternational.com

Scripture quotations (unless indicated otherwise) are from the English Standard Version Bible (ESV).

Cover design and interior layout by MiblArt.

FOREWORD

Who are you? would be a question you might ask meeting someone for the first time, especially if he or she were a stranger. The typical answer would be the person's name, but there is so much more to identity than a name.

Chances are Mark McKeehan is not a stranger to you. Maybe you have been on one of the baseball or basketball teams that he has coached. Or maybe you have heard him preach in person or online. Mark may have assisted you with life coaching or counseling.

I have gotten to know Mark over the past decade and have been inspired by his preaching and leadership gifts. In the last few years, that respect has increased as he became a board member of Grace Fellowship International, especially since he left the pastorate to become Executive Director in 2022. Whether serving together in Tennessee or on a ministry trip in the U.S. or overseas, I have seen firsthand that Mark is the "real deal."

One of Mark's outstanding qualities is *enthusiasm*. Whether he is talking about his wife, Carrie, their children, or a new idea for pioneering and engineering Christ-centered ministry, he is zealous. Does this include his enjoyment of coffee and celebration of the University of Tennessee's baseball team winning the national championship this year? Yes! By the way, the word "enthusiasm" comes from the Greek word, *entheos*, from the roots *en* (in) and *theos* (God). Thankfully, Mark has the Spirit of God as his source of zeal for the gospel, discipleship, and "equipping the saints" (Eph. 4:12).

His ministry draws from a variety of life experiences, roles, and relationships. In these pages, you'll get glimpses of Mark's role as husband, father, athlete, coach, pastor, missionary, life coach, and more. But if you were to ask him about his identity, he would especially want you to know how much the lessons presented in this book have guided him in answering that question biblically and confidently.

If he were still with us, the founder of GFI, Charles Solomon, would underline the importance of the believer's union with Christ as it relates to identity. Galatians 2:20 says it so well: "I have been crucified with Christ; it is no longer I who live, but Christ lives in me; and the life which I now live in the flesh I live by faith in the Son of God, who loved me and gave Himself for me."

When your identity flows from your experience of *identification with Jesus Christ*, it is not only inspirational but transformational.

In the years of being a baseball pitcher, Mark would be eager to head to the mound and get the game started. And now he waves us out of the dugout to join him in this exploration of your identity. A great "cloud of witnesses" (Heb. 12:1) are in the stands, cheering us on, so let's go!

Foreword

John Woodward M.Div, D.Min
Director of Counseling and Training
Grace Fellowship International

TABLE OF CONTENTS

Note from the author vii

Introduction viii

Chapter One 1

Chapter Two 7

Chapter Three................................ 12

Chapter Four 19

Chapter Five................................. 27

Chapter Six 35

Chapter Seven.............................. 43

Chapter Eight 48

Chapter Nine 58

Chapter Ten 65

Publisher's Appendix 69

NOTE FROM THE AUTHOR

Years ago, my friend Trevor and I were on our way to go hunting. We had been having great conversations, when suddenly, out of nowhere, he said to me, "You do something, and it is driving me crazy." That's a way to change the tone of the trip! Of course, I was curious as to what he would say next. Trevor said, "Why do you say Holy Spirit? Most people say *the* Holy Spirit." I laughed and said, "Well, I do not say the God or the Jesus." To be honest, I do not know when or even why I dropped "the" from Holy Spirit. The more I learned of the Spirit, the closer our relationship became. I do not write this to urge you to do the same. I want you to know I did not add "the" to Holy Spirit for the purpose of this book. There are many "red lines" in my manuscript as Microsoft Word is telling me I am wrong. I hope by the end of this book you will understand why.

All Scripture references in the book are taken from the English Standard Version unless otherwise noted.

INTRODUCTION

Who do you think you are? Ask yourself that question several times in different ways. Depending on how you say it, or who is asking, that question will put you on the offensive or cause you to think. My prayer is for you to consider that question deeply. So, let me ask you again, "Who are you?" You may wonder why this question is necessary. This question is asking us to consider our identity, and this is an important question for us to ponder. Why? Our identity drives not just who we are but also what we do. This question is so important, and it is probably why you picked up this book (and I am grateful!).

Years ago, I asked myself this same question because the things I saw in my life didn't match what I wanted. I wanted victory and joy (I read they were available in the Scriptures) and even though they were sometimes my experiences, victory and joy were not the default of life for me. I would come home from work and my wife would ask me, "How was your day?" I always felt like I said the same thing over and over, but it never seemed to be a "good day." Why? My life was not terrible, and many good things were happening all around me. My marriage was great, my children were blessings, and our church was growing. As I thought and prayed, I knew the truth. The

Introduction

problem was me! This journey led me back to my original question, "Who am I?"

I want to take you on a journey to find out who you are. I mean, isn't that the age-old question? How many times have we thought, "Who am I and why am I here on earth?" You may be surprised that many people live with a false identity. Living with a false identity is a recipe for a defeated life. In the Gospel of John 10:10, Jesus says, *"The thief comes only to steal and kill and destroy. I came that they may have life and have it abundantly."* We believe the first part but what about the second? Most Christians believe there is an enemy. We have been to church enough times to hear about Satan and demons, but an abundant life, for many, seems only to be a dream. A lot of people think this "abundant life" is what comes only in Heaven. It will take another book to break that down, but the abundant life is available today, right now, to all believers! How? Think of the life of Christ. Would you agree the life of Christ is eternal, victorious, and abundant? I would, and the Scriptures agree. OK, now think of your life. Would you agree that your life is eternal, victorious, and abundant? If you are like most people I speak to, you either shake your head "no" or choose not to say anything. The truth is, your life, the spiritual life in you, is eternal, victorious, and abundant if you are in Christ and Christ is in you! This is the beauty of what Paul teaches us throughout his Epistles. In Colossians 1, Paul is discussing his ministry to the church. Then he writes,

"To them, God chose to make known how great among the Gentiles are the riches of the glory of this mystery, which is Christ in you, the hope of glory."

Christ, who is eternal, victorious, and abundant, is in you right now if you have been born again. This truth means you have a life that is eternal, victorious, and abundant! You may not *feel* like this is true, but you are called to live in truth, not feelings.

Here is our problem! If our life is defined like this, then why are my experiences in life different than the truth I see in Scripture? We define life through circumstances, and we seek emotions over truth. Good things make me happy and bad things make me mad or sad. If we are honest, one bad thing makes the entire day terrible! Because of this truth, I started changing my vocabulary years ago and telling my wife my day had good moments and some bad ones. Words matter, and using the correct ones, coupled with the correct beliefs, changes our outcomes. For example, let's say you and I are neighbors and went out for coffee, and it was a great time. We laughed and had a deep conversation that left both of us uplifted and edified. But after coffee, I had a few bad things happen. Maybe it was a bad counseling appointment and an email that hurt my feelings. I arrive home, get out of the car, and you are outside and overhear my wife ask, "Honey, how was your day?" I say, "Terrible, it was a terrible day!" What would you think? You would conclude, "Wow, I thought coffee this morning was great, but I guess I was wrong." You may go inside pondering and, without knowing it, get bitter towards me. Days later, I may ask you to go to coffee again and you refuse. I ask questions, you get short with me, and I start questioning, "What in the world happened? Did I say something wrong at coffee the other morning? That was such a great time together."

Introduction

Do you see the problem? I had some bad moments that day but if I lump them together, I miss all the good things that happened. Now, what does this have to do with identity? Too many people have tied in their identity with performance. For example, we falsely believe my bad days happen because I am bad. My business failed because I was a failure. This leads us to say things like, "I am not smart enough," and leaves us feeling insecure, inadequate, and feeling inferior. This journey to biblical identity is so important.

Thank you for allowing me to be your "Guide." At Grace Fellowship International, where I work as a life coach and the Executive Director, we chose the word "Guide" to use for all our counselors. I love this word for two reasons. For one, a guide is someone who helps you get to a place you cannot get to on your own. For example, if you want to climb a high mountain or travel somewhere deep into the jungle, you get a guide. These guides have made the journey before, so you trust the guide will lead you safely to the place you are aiming to go. But a guide does another important thing; they point out things along the way that you might otherwise miss. On the way, you are mesmerized by the beauty, but the guide stops and points out the things they know you do not want to miss. I am excited to be your guide throughout this journey to find our true biblical identity.

Before we start, I am not going to tell you to put your arms and legs inside the vehicle, but I do want to tell you this journey has helped me live in daily victory. I say that because no one wants a guide if it is the guide's first time out. How scary would that be? You are nervous and you begin the climb and ask "How many times have you done this climb?" You are hoping for a large number and the answer back is, "This is my first time out!" I am not perfect, but I do want to help guide you into a complete and victorious identity in Christ.

These pages flow out of my counseling and coaching sessions, and I am grateful for what the Lord has taught me through these many conversations. In this book, I would like to share these thoughts and lessons with you. Are you ready for a grace discipleship adventure? Let's go!

CHAPTER ONE

"Would you tell me a little about yourself?" This question is often asked by people who are just meeting for the first time or by two people wanting to know more about each other. This question, however, gets confused with identity. If you ask me this question, I may answer without thinking, "I am a husband, a father, a son, an uncle, a nephew, a coach, and the Executive Director of Grace Fellowship International." As we talk, I may add, "I was a pastor for over 25 years, I played baseball in college, and I am currently an assistant coach for a boys high school team."

This is not *who* I am; these statements describe things about me. This information is helpful for you to get to know me and to understand me, but it is not foundational. I am not building my life upon statements such as pastor, coach, or even husband, although I love aspects of each of them. I love being a husband to my wife, and I love being a father to my five children. I enjoy coaching, and working at GFI doesn't feel like work because I am so fulfilled in the work. I say this because there is nothing wrong with descriptors, but that is what they are, nothing more.

Many people walk around using *descriptors* as *identifiers*. The problem, however, is these descriptors can change for the better or the worse. Years ago, before I was an assistant basketball coach, I walked into the high school and was known as "Brycen's dad." Brycen is my oldest son, and he played basketball at the high school. When my daughter started school, depending on whom I saw at the high school, I may also be "Regan's dad." The coach at the time asked me to become a chaplain, so my title went from "Brycen's dad" to "Pastor Mark." If you walk in with me today, you will hear the boys say, "Hey, Coach Mark!" Over the years my *descriptors* changed, but I *stayed* the same.

The difference between descriptors and identifiers is so important, and I want to tell you why. If you use the words above or different ones of your choosing to be your identity, what happens when one of those changes or is taken away? I mentioned I played college baseball. What I should probably say is that I was on the team. I played for a small DIII school in my hometown of Maryville, TN. My senior year seemed to be going well. I was a starting pitcher with a 4-1 record. I was warming up and getting ready to start the game. Everything was normal, and I remember talking with my coach about the lead-off batter for the opposing team. He loved first-pitch fastballs, and if I remember correctly, he had 9 homeruns off first-pitch fastballs. Of course, I didn't want to be #10 so I started him off with a curve ball.

I remember two things vividly. First, a shock of pain went through my entire right arm. The second was watching the ball float toward the batter without curving. Then I watched this lead-off batter stand on third base after hitting a first-pitch triple. Hey, at least it wasn't a homerun! This was followed by my coach yelling and screaming at me.

Chapter One

It was at this moment that I realized I could not lift my arm. I would find out a few days later that my injury to my pitching arm would end my baseball career, and baseball at this time *was* my identity.

I started playing baseball when I was 4 years old. My dad had me out in the yard not long after I had started walking and could swing a little bat. You see, at this time, my identity was baseball player. There were so many nights that everyone in my family's schedule conformed to what time I had practice or the time of my game. Shoney's and McDonald's, along with the concession stand, became our family table for dinner. But now, it was gone, finished, and to be honest, I did not know what to do. For the next few days, I walked around like someone had died; the truth is a part of me *had* died. I remember asking my parents if I should go to class. It seems crazy to say today, but I was confused and did not know what to do because I no longer knew who I was! The *one* thing I had placed my identity in was now gone forever.

This one was hard for me, but life hits with harder lessons. What if your identity is as a husband and your wife passes away? What if your identity is as a mom and you lose a child? Even with a true biblical identity, this would be beyond hard, but when you add a false identity, you do not lose one thing; you lose everything. Descriptors describe; they tell others about what I do, and what I have, and they give information about me, but it is God who defines me. This is true for you also. Christ alone gives you your identity.

Why is this so important? I have heard people say things like, "You are what you eat." I guess that means if you eat unhealthily, then you are on the path to unhealthiness. However, I do know this is true: "You are what you think!" But what if what you think is wrong? Paul closes a powerful letter to the Romans by saying in Romans 12:2,

"Do not be conformed to this world, but be transformed by the renewal of your mind, that by testing you may discern what is the will of God, what is good and acceptable and perfect."

The world agrees you are what you think! There are so many books on positive thinking, and do not get me wrong, I am all about thinking positively. But positive thinking alone doesn't give you a true, biblical identity. The world says you are what you have. What do we call those with a lot of stuff? It is not a trick question. We call them "rich." Those without a lot or the opposite of rich we call "poor." In fact, in the world, we label people based on what they do and what we think of them. What you eat, what you smell like, and even what kind of vehicle you drive makes people think certain things about you. "You do not eat meat? Oh, you are one of those people. All you eat is meat, then you live on crazy fad diets!" We call people athletes because they play sports, or after we watch them play, we say they think they are an athlete. We call people names based on what they wear, how they act, or based on how they sound. If you met me and heard me speak, you may call me a "hillbilly" or "redneck" just because I have a southern East Tennessee accent. A lot of

Chapter One

people in this world have been hurt because of the *labels* given to them by someone else.

There is a statistic I read and, at first, I did not believe it. I began listening to my thoughts and asking others. Then I believed it was true! What is the statistic? Charlotte Johnson, MA, LPCC writes, "For some reason, our brains defer to the negative. According to the National Science Foundation, 80% of our thoughts are negative and 95% of our thoughts are repetitive." You may wonder how many thoughts do we have a day? Charlotte continues, "Researchers at Queen's University in Canada estimated that we have 6,200 thoughts every day."[1]

When I first heard this, I shared it with a church staff I was speaking to. When I made the claim, I noticed several of the pastors shaking their heads and looking confused. At lunch, one of them asked me about the stat and challenged its validity. I looked at him and said, "Since we left for lunch, you have made eight negative statements, mostly about yourself and your ministry." No joke, he looked at me and said, "Well, I guess I am just stupid!" I just answered and said, "That's nine!"

I'm not good at math, but eighty percent of 6,200 is 4,960 negative thoughts per day! That is a lot of negativity! This means the things we think and say about ourselves are wrong. Honestly, do you walk around saying to yourself, "Man, I am dominating this day." Or do you say things like "I am terrible. I stink at this. Everyone else is better at this than me." I bet the latter is true, and based on the stats, it is!

Positive thinking may help a little, but Paul says it is transformational thinking that changes things. "Do not be like the world but be transformed"(Romans 12:2). How? By renewing your mind. Think about truthful things! This is what I want to help you to do.

---

[1] https://care-clinics.com/stuck-on-negative-thinking/#:~:text=For%20some%20reason%2C%20our%20brains,of%20our%20thoughts%20are%20repetitive.

CHAPTER TWO

"Come on, boy, let's see what you are made of!" I cannot tell you how often I have heard a coach say this to me or someone on my team. That question was usually followed by a hard task meant to help us become *stronger*. Maybe it was just for the coaches to get a good laugh or to punish us, but sometimes it did the opposite of making us stronger! However, this is a question we all seem to ponder at some point. Today our world is in the midst of an identity crisis. Webster's Dictionary defines an *identity crisis* as a "personal psychosocial conflict, especially in adolescence that involves confusion about one's social role and often a sense of loss of continuity to one's personality."[2]

Think about all the movies that picture this conflict. How many times have we viewed people who go on a search to find themselves? Many of these movies portray this as a journey, a quest that brings them back with something they didn't possess when they left. Does anyone remember the movie, "The Truman Show?" It stars Jim Carey as a man named Truman who lived what he thought was a normal life in a normal city. What he didn't know was that everything was being filmed, and his entire life was a TV show watched by the whole world! "AALLRRIIGGHHTTYY then!" Sorry, that quote was from the wrong movie, but I couldn't help myself! As an adult, Truman begins to unravel the truth, and for the rest of the movie, he struggles and strives for personal freedom.

Most people are looking for their identity in the wrong place and in the wrong people. We see this a lot in children. They look to their peers for identity. They dress and act in certain ways in hopes of being a part of a certain group of people they want to be associated with. Teenagers will act a certain way at school but be different at home or church. Teenagers look to other teenagers for their identity. However, we need to think about this fact: teenagers who do not have fully completed brains are looking for acceptance from others who, like them, do not have fully completed brains. This is creating a lot of issues in the world. Gavin Mackay writes, "It is well established that the brain undergoes a "rewiring" process that is not complete until approximately 25 years of age."[3]

Adults, however, are no different. We go into debt to purchase things we do not need, and if we are honest, we often do not even want them. Why? To be accepted and fit in. Our house must be clean before guests arrive because people will *label* us as lazy or unclean. We cannot run to the store without getting ready because what if we see someone we know?

Social media has made this pursuit of identity worse. I could quote stats, but I think you know I am telling you the truth. How many times have you posted something and then kept going back to look to see how many *likes* you received? To be more truthful, sometimes we even get mad that a silly post gets more views and likes than a serious

Chapter Two

one. When I was a pastor, Easter Sunday was one of the best and worst days of the year for me. It was the best for most of the reasons you can imagine. Most people in the church invite people to church for Easter, so churches see a lot of new people, and many of those people give their life to Christ. Our staff at the church I pastored always did such a fantastic job! So, in many ways, it was a great day!

However, I would go home, log on to social media, and play the comparison game. I remember years ago having a great day on Easter morning. We had set some goals for the weekend and blew them all away. Our team had done an amazing job in every area. We had a lot of new people, and we had people who had accepted Christ. I felt like I floated home. I had a great lunch with the family, and then it all went downhill. I logged on to a certain platform that I am no longer on and there it was. A church I followed gave the number of people saved and the number was more than people who attended our Easter service! I should have rejoiced because we are all on the same team. But I didn't; I complained! I felt sorry for myself and thought if I were a better communicator, a better planner, and a better pastor, then maybe our church would be better also. I was defeated. I forgot everything good that happened that morning. Why? My identity was in the number. I would have never said that, but what other reason could there be for me to get so defeated so quickly?

From there things did not get better; they got worse. I would define the effectiveness of my sermons based on whether people responded. If people came to the altar and prayed, then I must have preached a good sermon.

If not, I failed. Here is the problem with false identities; failing makes you believe you are a failure. If you live as a failure, then you come to expect failure, because that is who you are!

This didn't just happen on Sundays but crept in on Mondays too. Usually, midafternoon I would receive an email from our financial director giving us the total donations taken in from the day before. People attending church hate hearing about money, but honestly, you must bring in money to pay the bills. During this time of ministry for me, many Mondays we did not bring in what we needed to be in a healthy place. But here was the issue for me; if the email was good, meaning we made the budget, I thought of myself as a good leader. But when we didn't make the budget, I blamed myself. I would think to myself, "This church needs a better pastor, someone who teaches them the Word and helps them get in a better place." Then I would drown my sorrows away eating a cheeseburger.

We all deal with stress differently, and mine was food. This is why they call it "comfort food." On Mondays, if things were bad, I would call the lady who owned the restaurant across the street from our church. I would walk over to a plate full of fries and a huge and very tasty cheeseburger. I would be halfway done when I realized I had already eaten lunch! I was not hungry; I was stressed. That cheeseburger had become my "God of Comfort." Because my identity was wrong, my stress plan was wrong. I did not run to Christ; I walked over to eat! Do this for years and you gain over 60 pounds like I did. I do not have

Chapter Two

to tell you, but adding on an extra 60 pounds didn't help my false identity. It made things worse.

I have a friend who is a former professional athlete. I remember my wife and I watching him perform one Sunday, and he did great! We were cheering, and I got on social media to see so many people, like me, cheering him on. All the posts were supportive and encouraging. The next week he wrecked, and again, I got on social media. However, this time people were mean, negative, and posting things that made me so mad! I wanted to answer them all and even tell some people what they could do! During this season, he and I would have a phone call on Thursday mornings. On one of those morning calls, I asked him, "How do you do it? How do you post and read the comments that are so up and down?" Do you know what he said? "Mark, I do not allow people to tell me that I am great or horrible. I know who I am." Then he added, "I think you need to start doing the same." That was such a life-changing lesson. I also want to thank him for helping me lose over 60 pounds.

Before I lost the weight, however, I came to my identity crisis. It was another Easter in 2015, and I stood in front of the mirror wondering who this person was I was looking at. Can I be honest? I didn't like him, and I knew I needed a change. That was the day I started my journey.

---

[2] https://www.merriam-webster.com/dictionary/identity%20crisis

[3] https://www.ncbi.nlm.nih.gov/pmc/articles/PMC3621648/

CHAPTER THREE

My journey took me to two places. One was to God's Word, and the other was to a place. First, let me start with the place. I took a sabbatical from the church I pastored in the summer of 2015. I could no longer continue living the way I was living. The leadership of my church was amazing and graciously allowed me to take the time I needed to get healthy. I often tell people that I wasn't burned out, but I was on the road heading toward burnout, and I didn't want to take that exit! I had seen too many people go that way before, and none of them returned the same! I thought about all the people who, through burnout, lost their spouse, their ministry, their passion, and some lost their lives.

As I was planning my time away, I prayed God would make my time powerful, intimate, and purposeful. It was then that my (now) mentor, Hans Haun asked me to go to Grace Fellowship International. I met Dr. Charles Solomon, the founder of GFI, and I began reading his foundational book, *Handbook to Happiness*. This resource has helped members of the body of Christ to experience, mature in, and effectively communicate the message of identification with Christ in His death, burial, resurrection, and ascension in their various spheres of influence, so that

Chapter Three

all may know Christ as Savior, Lord, and Life.[4] The website of GFI (www.GraceFellowshipInternational.com) states that since 1970, GFI has been helping "disciplers" to live victoriously, disciple strategically, and counsel effectively. GFI is built on Galatians 2:20, which says,

"I have been crucified with Christ and I no longer live, but Christ lives in me. The life I now live in the body, I live by faith in the Son of God, who loved me and gave himself for me (NIV)."

I learned several things that day that began to change the way I thought, and it also changed the way I would live. What did I learn? First, Jesus is not just my Lord and Savior; He is also my Life. This is what Paul writes in Galatians 2:20, "*I was crucified with Christ, and I no longer live.*" The life I am living now is Christ's life in and through me. After Jesus died, he was buried, and spiritually, I was buried also. When he arose, I arose also as a new creation. I am not who I once was. Before we come to Christ, Paul states,

"And you were dead in the trespasses and sins in which you once walked, following the course of this world, following the prince of the power of the air, the spirit that is now at work in the sons of disobedience, among whom we all once lived in the passions of our flesh, carrying out the desires of the body and the mind, and were by nature children of wrath, like the rest of mankind" (Ephesians 2:1–3).

The good news, which begins in v. 4, says,

"But God, being rich in mercy, because of the great love with which He loved us, even when we were dead in our trespasses, made us alive together with Christ—by grace you have been saved and raised us up with Him and seated us with Him in the heavenly places in Christ Jesus (Ephesians 2:4–6, ESV)."

Christ has made us new, and He has given us life! He has made us sit with Him in the heavenly places, but more on that in the chapters to come.

At GFI, I met a man named Rob Clogg who first walked me through the wheel and line diagrams, made known through Dr. Solomon's book, *Handbook to Happiness* (I recommend this book, and if nothing else, please get a copy and read Chapter 1 & 2). I learned more fully what is known as the *Exchanged Life*. In the wheel diagram, we see how life works when flesh (that is another way of saying self-life) is in complete control. The flesh can be defined as acting independently of God. Basically, it is doing what we want, when we want, and how we want. When we live this way, we tend to view life, especially problems and issues, through a tornado lens of emotion (even as believers).

What do I mean by that? When issues arise and I am in the center of my own life, I get worried, and my worry stirs up doubt and fear. Then the more I doubt and fear, the more I worry. Thus, the tornado begins but it quickly goes from an F1 to an F5 by adding feelings of inferiority, feelings of inadequacy, and feelings of insecurity. Oh, then throw some guilt on for good measure. These emotions arise out of me, so when I am my own functional source of living, I cannot live any other way.

Chapter Three

As all this outside trouble comes in, what comes out is a *hostile reaction*. I use the word "reaction," because it is quick, without thought or prayer. This hostility causes us to either blow up or clam up. Blowing up is all about our attitudes and actions, including but not limited to abuse and addictions. This explains why people in their stress yell, hit or throw things, or just go get drunk to try and escape the issues of life. We clam up, or we could say we just shut down in our minds or our emotions. In our minds, we clam up in fantasy, paranoia, or obsessions. Maybe the way we see this most is in binge-watching shows. Now I am not against TV or watching several episodes in one sitting. Think of people who, after a stressful day, go home, turn on the TV, and watch it until they fall asleep. Then they repeat the same cycle the very next day. If we run to the TV/show before Christ, then that's a sin. We are trusting that show instead of Jesus. Our TV show, just like food was for me, can become our god of comfort!

We clam up in our emotions, which produces depression and anxiety. This is not the book to dive deep into it, but consider that in its most simplistic form, depression is the fear of yesterday, anxiety is the fear of tomorrow, and insecurity, inadequacy, and inferiority are the fears of today. Anxiety and depression begin when we are the center of our own lives, trying to live out what God wants to live out through us.

If your identity is based on self, then this is the only way you know to live. The message of the Exchanged Life asks, "What would it look like if you exchanged your self-life for Christ's life?" Remember that I said, based on Galatians 2:20, that Jesus is our Lord, Savior, and Life.

When you look at life and the problems of life through the lens of Christ, things change. Jesus didn't worry, and He had no doubts or fears. He never felt inferior, or inadequate, nor was He insecure. He didn't experience guilt because He never sinned. I know you may be thinking, "Mark, I am not God!" No, you are not, but He is in you! Listen to what Paul writes in the first few verses of Colossians 3,

*"If then you have been raised with Christ, seek the things that are above, where Christ is, seated at the right hand of God. Set your mind on the things that are above, not on things that are on earth. For you have died, and **your life is hidden with Christ in God. When Christ who is your life** appears, then you also will appear with Him in glory* (ESV)."

Because Christ is your life, you are a new creation. Notice these truths about you from scripture: 1 Corinthians 2:16 ends by stating *"We have the mind of Christ."* May I ask you a question? If you have the mind of Christ, why would you ever use yours? We have a limited perspective and limited resources, but God is unlimited and all-powerful. He sees the beginning and the end. Even with this truth, you still choose to use your limited thinking, and so do I. I am not saying that you are not smart, but our thinking can lead us to depression, anxiety, and fear. Again, these emotions arise out of our own limited and finite minds and thoughts. But remember, we have His mind so we should not desire to think independently

Chapter Three

of God. Everything Jesus does is good, just, and perfect. Therefore, we should ask Him what we are to do, what we are to say, and how should we think of this situation. When we surrender and allow Him to work through us, then the works He produces through us will also be good, just, and powerful! Paul writes in Philippians 4:7 that we have the peace of Christ: *"And the peace of God, which surpasses all understanding, will guard your hearts and your minds in Christ Jesus."* Then in verse 9 he adds, *"What you have learned and received and heard and seen in me practice these things, and the God of peace will be with you."* Let me give you one more; Philippians 4:13 tells us that we have the strength of Christ: *"I can do all things through Him who strengthens me."*

With Christ in me and working through me, I can have a godly response through Christ, not a hostile reaction. A *response* is something we have thought through and prayed about. With Christ in me, I do not react by blowing up, and I do not clam up; I *respond* with love, joy, peace, kindness, gentleness, long-suffering, and with self-control. With Christ in me, He produces the Fruit of the Spirit in and through me.

I know you probably have questions. I went through that really quickly, and there is a lot more to teach and learn. We use this and more in our counseling and life coaching at Grace Fellowship International.[5]

Finally, I met Dr. John Woodward. Little did I know this meeting would change my life and my career. Outside of my mentor, Hans, Dr. John has taught me more about the Exchanged Life and identity than anyone else. When

I came back from my sabbatical, I had Dr. John come and teach on the Exchanged Life twice. Years later, I joined the board of GFI, and in 2022, through a series of crazy but divine events, I left my church and became the Executive Director of GFI. I get the honor and privilege to walk alongside Dr. John, guiding people into a complete and victorious identity in Christ every day. In the next chapter, we will consider how my sabbatical study of God's word led to a new appreciation of our identity in Christ.

---

[4] https://gracefellowshipinternational.com

[5] You can learn more about who we are and what we do at GFI's website: www.GraceFellowshipInternational.com. If you want and or need counseling or life coaching, please send an email to hello@gracefellowshipinternational.com.

CHAPTER FOUR

I mentioned the first place my journey sent me was to God's Word. The Word is more than just letters in the pages of a divine book we call the Bible. The Word is Christ, and John tells us in John 1:1–3,

"In the beginning was the Word, and the Word was with God, and the Word was God. He was in the beginning with God. All things were made through Him, and without Him was not anything made that was made." John adds an additional truth in verse 14, *"And the Word became flesh and dwelt among us, and we have seen His glory, glory as of the only Son from the Father, full of grace and truth."*

In Matthew 16:13–17, Jesus takes the disciples to a place called Caesarea Philippi, located twenty-five miles north of Capernaum. This was a fertile place and thus became attractive for religious worship. Numerous temples were built in this area. This was an evil place full of human sacrifices and temple prostitution.

Stuart K. Weber writes in the *Holman New Testament Commentary* on Matthew, "Caesarea Philippi was a quiet place at the headwaters of the Jordan River, a place long associated with idol worship and pagan deities. Standing beneath the idols of a so-called deity, Pan (mentioned in classical writings as a seer, fortune teller, and a giver of revelations), carved into the cliffside, Jesus knew the timing was right to raise and settle the question of His identity."[6]

This is not a place you might expect to find Jesus and His disciples, but it is here in Caesarea Philippi that Jesus asks his disciples a question, *"Who do people say that the Son of Man is?"* (Matthew 16:13). Weber adds, "Jesus apparently had to ask his first question of the disciples more than once (asked is in the imperfect Greek tense, and delivers the meaning, 'he asked repeatedly').[7] This is a good question, and I love how Jesus answers the question within the question he asks them. Look at it again. He doesn't just ask them who people say that He is. He says, "Who do people say that the *Son of Man* is?" Do you see? He answers the question within the question. He is the Son of Man! In verse 14, they answer, *"Some say John the Baptist, others say Elijah, and others Jeremiah or one of the prophets."*

Often in counseling and life coaching, I walk people through this question. The disciples answered Jesus' question with the answers they had heard. Jesus had performed miracles, and He had spoken with authority. No doubt there was a lot being said about who He was, so the disciples repeated back to Jesus what they had heard. Let me ask you something: what do people say about you? Think about this for a moment. Maybe you might want to write down some of these words in the margin. Most people answer with words such as "kind," "loyal," "fun," "easy to talk to," "loving," or words they have heard from others.[8]

Chapter Four

However, sometimes the words we have heard are not good ones. Some used words like "traitor," "abuser," "mean," "angry," "deceitful," or "adulterer." Dr. Woodward and I were in South Africa, and we had the privilege to speak to a group of men who had been rescued and saved from street life. These guys had all sorts of different backgrounds, but they had one thing in common. All of them had given their life to Christ! When I asked the question, "What do people say about you?" they replied with statements such as, "thief," "drug user", and "lost cause." This was sad to hear, but let's be honest, most of us are wearing an *invisible name tag given to us by someone else.*

How many of you are living with a false identity that *you* have given yourself? You *did* something bad and now you *think* you are bad. Maybe you tried something and failed, so you wear the name tag of *"failure."* Maybe you have been successful, and you are wearing the name tag of *"success,"* which isn't beneficial. You may call yourself by the sin you committed, but that is a name tag given to you by yourself or the enemy, not Christ!

Back in Matthew 16, Jesus doesn't stop there with the disciples. In verse 15, He asks them another question, and this question is more personal; *"But who do you say that I am?"* Now, Jesus is not just interested in what the disciples have heard, He wants to know what they thought. Peter replies, *"You are the Christ, the Son of the Living God."* After I ask people to tell me what others think of them, I ask them this same question: "What do you say about yourself?" But then I follow with this question, "Do you believe in what others say about you?"

Many times, people will answer and say they do indeed believe what others say. They may try to be humbler. Some people do not want to come across as self-righteous, while others do not want anyone to know *anything* about themselves. They are a closed book, which many times is the result of rejections within relationships in their past. Others get honest here and they start confessing to things they are struggling with, things that have led them to contact GFI. You see, it is interesting that we define ourselves with what we *do*. I identified as a baseball player because that is what I *did*. When that was taken away, I didn't know what I was supposed to do. Your essential identity comes from nothing or no one else but the Word, Jesus Christ.

I have the honor to do life coaching with some amazing people. One of those is my pastor, Cory Lethgo. When I resigned from being a lead pastor, my family and I sought a new church. God is so good, and He led us to our church, River Stone Church, located in Knoxville, TN. We love our new church and our faith community. I love being able to coach my pastor, but I also love being taught the Scriptures *by* him. One Sunday, Pastor Cory was teaching about identity, and he stated that our identity isn't based on *popularity*, *possessions*, or *potential*. I would add that our identity isn't based on *positions* or our *profession* either. These are lies sold to us by the flesh and the enemy! Let's dive into these issues a bit deeper, shall we?

Everyone wants to be *known* by someone. I'm sure someone will read this and say they are a loner and love being alone, but I bet there is a moment, even for that person, that they wish to be known, really known, by

Chapter Four

someone. This starts early in school. We walk in and immediately start looking for people who are like us, people who like what we like, and people who are for what we are for. This doesn't change as we get older; it just becomes more difficult.

When it comes to identity, we are not defined by *popularity*, or by how many friends we have. Sometimes when we discuss this with clients, they will say, "I wasn't as popular as this person." What does that mean? Better yet, why does that matter? It matters to some people because they believe the more friends they have, the better or more valuable person they must be. I think we all know that is not true, but our flesh and the enemy want us to believe otherwise! Having friends or being popular isn't what defines us. The opposite is also not true. Being a loner or having no friends doesn't define you. It describes your social life and activities calendar, but that is not who you are!

"*He who dies with the most toys still dies*." I believe my dad had this motto on a shirt when I was a teenager. It was from the brand "*No Fear*." Another lie about our identity is that we are defined by our *possessions*, either by what we have accumulated or by what we lack. This person has a lot of stuff so they must be cool and rich or maybe they are impulsive and in debt. We are not defined by what we have, and this is important. If we are defined by things, then what happens when the thing breaks, is stolen, or no longer validates us? How many times have we heard someone say, "If only I had this new car, a bigger home, etc., then my life would be better."? Jesus taught that we are not to lay up treasures here on earth but in heaven. In Matthew 6:19–21, Jesus teaches,

"Do not lay up for yourselves treasures on earth, where moth and rust destroy and where thieves break in and steal, but lay up for yourselves treasures in heaven, where neither moth nor rust destroys and where thieves do not break in and steal. For where your treasure is, there your heart will be also."

At Grace Fellowship International, we love to say your heart is the center of who you are; it is your functional source of living. Whatever you place in the center of your heart is the lens by which you view everything else. If you identify with stuff, then what will you do when those thieves break in and steal, or time makes it rot and break? Think about it: not only will you have lost your "*thing*" but also a part of your identity.

Sometimes, right here, people begin to think, "Ok, now I have to do better!" "I need to work harder!" You will hopefully see things clearer in the chapters to come, but your identity is not in your *potential*. Jesus didn't save you for what He thinks you will do for Him sometime in the future. I don't want you to believe that you are lacking things and that, hopefully, you will find them by the time you finish reading this book. You have it all right now! In Christ, you lack *nothing*! If you don't believe me, then lay this book down and go read two verses for me. The first one is Ephesians 1:3, and the second is Colossians 2:10. I will dive into these in the chapters to come, but Paul tells us two things here. First, we have been blessed with every spiritual blessing in the heavenly places. This means we lack *nothing*! The second states that we are *complete* in Christ! God did not choose us based on our potential. He doesn't *need* you and me; He chooses to allow us to participate and cooperate with Him.

Your identity is different than your *profession*. You are not identified as a manager, teacher, pastor, or whatever you do for a living. Again, your profession describes what you do. It gives us a little more information about you. I love what I do for a living, and like you, I have worked hard for years to achieve this position. I am not minimizing our work, but we need to put our vocations into proper perspective.

Titles are not identity. Think of all the titles you've had. I have had the titles of son, baseball player, brother, uncle, pastor, executive director, and some others that I cannot put in this book. Some titles, or should I say labels, hurt, don't they? For Christmas a few years ago, my son Hudson bought me a piece of land in Ireland. Ok, it was a 1x1 foot piece of land, but the gesture was very thoughtful. By purchasing a piece of land in Ireland through a particular website, one is considered a "lord." It was fun for a few days to be "Lord Dad," or some friends hopped on and called me "Lord Mark." Corbin, another one of my sons, said to me during our fun, "Dad, you are not the LORD!" I agreed and said, "I am not the LORD, but I am a lord in Kerry, Ireland." He disagreed, stating, "There is only one LORD, and His name is Jesus. You, Dad, are not the LORD!" He didn't see the fun! Like I said, titles come and go. Kids are great to help make us humbler.

Who Do You Think You Are?

I think we have missed the point as well. We think titles *define* us as leaders or titles *give* us our identity. Both are incorrect! We all have had bosses that have titles and are not good leaders. But again, if you identify as a leader and that title is removed, then you lose more than a job, a promotion, and/or money.

I do want to visit Kerry, Ireland, and find my 1x1 foot parcel of land. I just want to walk through a field and imagine taking everyone else's land who paid the $25 to become a lord. They will not even know I took their title and changed my title to "Mark, the Conqueror! King of the ones who fell for the gimmick!" It is fun, so I made Hudson and my dad both "lords in Ireland" as well!

What does the Bible say about you? Let's find out!

---

[6] Stuart K. Weber, "Holman New Testament Commentary: Matthew" 2000, Broadman & Holman Publishers, Nashville, TN, pages 248-249.

[7] Weber, pg. 249.

[8] This exposition is part of session one of GFI's "Finding Joy" seminar.

CHAPTER FIVE

Do you want to know how to get a big "AMEN" in church? Just state your name and say, "I am just a sinner saved by grace!" "Amen!" I do not know who started this saying, but that's a terrible identity! I am sorry if that hurts your feelings, but that is not who you are. That statement describes what happens when you first accept and believe in Christ. You *were* a sinner, and *you have been* saved by grace. Ephesians 2:1–3 again explains,

"And you were dead in the trespasses and sins in which you once walked, following the course of this world, following the prince of the power of the air, the spirit that is now at work in the sons of disobedience—among whom we all once lived in the passions of our flesh, carrying out the desires of the body and the mind, and were by nature children of wrath, like the rest of mankind."

You were a sinner, but if you are born again, you should not identify as a sinner anymore. I do not mean that you do not sin. I mean your *identity* is not "sinner." Why is that important? Let me ask you, "What do builders do?" Seriously, this is not a trick question. What do they do? They build! What do painters do? They paint! Recently, I was in Cape Town, South Africa, and watching surfers out in the Indian Ocean. My friend asked me if I wanted to try, but before I left America, I had watched "Shark Week" on the Discovery Channel. They were filming off an island filled with seals located behind these surfers! At a seminar where I was teaching, I asked these questions of identity; I said, "What do surfers do?" They answered, "Surf!" I corrected them and said, "No, they are the shark's buffet."

What about sinners? What do sinners do? They sin! When you sin, and you sometimes do, that goes against your new spiritual nature. It is not who you are but what you *choose* to do! However, if you choose to identify as a *sinner,* then when you *sin,* you will excuse it by saying this is just who I am. So, let's ask the question, "*Who am I?*"

Paul writes in Ephesians 1:1, "*Paul, an apostle of Christ Jesus by the will of God, to the saints who are in Ephesus, and are faithful in Christ Jesus.*" You are a saint! This is your true, biblical identity! "Nope, not me! I am not a saint." Why do you *say* or *think* that? Most people say, "Mark, I do not do saintly things." What are "saintly things" exactly? We must be very careful here. Are we saints if we spend a certain number of hours in prayer and Bible reading? Does this title mean I must be in full-time ministry or perform some kind of miraculous act? If you come from a Catholic background, you have been taught saints are those who have performed miracles. The Catholic definition says, "Saints are persons in heaven (officially canonized or not), who lived heroically virtuous lives, offered their life for others, or were martyred for the faith, and who are worthy of imitation. In official Church procedures,

Chapter Five

there are three steps to sainthood: a candidate becomes "Venerable," then "Blessed" and then "Saint." Venerable is the title given to a deceased person recognized formally by the pope as having lived a heroically virtuous life or offered their life. To be beatified and recognized as Blessed, one miracle acquired through the candidate's intercession is required in addition to recognition of heroic virtue or offering of life. Canonization requires a second miracle after beatification. The pope may waive these requirements. A miracle is not required prior to a martyr's beatification, but one is required before canonization."[9] I do not wish to be controversial nor to be offensive. The truth is this; you are a *saint* because God's Word says so. Jesus' finished work on the cross *made* you a saint. You are a miracle, and the salvation given to you through Christ is also a miracle!

Look at Ephesians 1:1 again. Paul addresses the believers in the church of Ephesus as "saints" from the beginning. He is not addressing them based on their popularity, possessions, potential, or positions. Look at Philippians 1:1: *"Paul and Timothy, servants of Christ Jesus, to all the saints in Christ Jesus who are at Philippi, with the overseers and deacons."* Here Paul addresses certain titles but links all believers in the church as "saints."

Colossians 1:1 states, *"Paul, an apostle of Christ Jesus by the will of God, and Timothy our brother, to the saints and faithful brothers in Christ at Colossae: grace to you and peace from God our Father."* Wait, do not skip past this. Paul separates *identity* from what they *do*. He calls them *saints* because that is their identity, *who they are*. He commends them for being "faithful brothers," which is what they *did*. They are not saints because they are faithful. They were only faithful through Christ, who lives within them. We will cover that in the next chapter. If this verse were just a greeting, Paul wouldn't have called them saints elsewhere. Look at 2 Thessalonians 1:10. Paul is writing about judgment and Christ's second coming, and he tells us, *"When he comes on that day to be glorified in his saints, and to be marveled at among all who have believed because our testimony to you was believed."* Being a saint isn't about works; it is accomplished through faith. Wait, I should restate this; it is about work, but not ours. Our being a saint is accomplished through the finished work of Jesus Christ on the cross.

My mentor, Hans, says, "Isn't it more than just the shedding of His blood and dying on the cross? Isn't it really about His entire life, that is, His stepping down out of Heaven and being clothed in the likeness and humility as a man where He carried out all righteousness as a man, bringing the positive aspect of the Law, righteousness, to you and I who have become partakers of His life. And then in His death and burial, our death to sin and death accomplished, doing away with the old man in us that separated us from God, so that we, in His resurrection, have the newness of life that is holy and righteous and beloved in His life."

If being a saint is about our works, then we have a problem in the New Testament. The church at Corinth was a wreck. For instance, if you read the book of First Corinthians, you will see what I mean. When you study the passage, you almost imagine he wrote the book for the

Chapter Five

contemporary church. Paul is describing what it means to live as a Christian in the midst of a non-Christian world. First Corinthians starts with,

"Paul, called by the will of God to be an apostle of Christ Jesus, and our brother Sosthenes. To the church of God that is in Corinth, to those sanctified in Christ Jesus, called to be saints together with all those who in every place call upon the name of our Lord Jesus Christ, both their Lord and ours" (1 Corinthians 1:1–2).

Again, read the letter, and you will notice that Paul blows them up! Well, not literally, but he does go on to tell them everything they are doing wrong. If he writes to correct them, and because he is doing so, then why not address them as hypocrites, immature believers, or something else negative? He calls them saints because that is their identity. If you are a believer in Christ, then that is who you are as well!

You are a saint, not because of what you *do*, but because of who Jesus *is*. Paul writes in First Corinthians 1:2, "*called to be saints,*" and he also states, "*who in every place (including where you are) call upon the name of the Lord Jesus Christ.*" I love this! When you were born again, yes, you were saved from hell, but you got more. A lot more! You became a *saint* at that very moment!

What would tomorrow look like if you began to live like a saint? You may fear people would call you self-righteous (and the truth is that some will). It is sad, but how many people read or actually *study* Scripture? It is right there in the Word of God. Living from a saintly identity is not self-righteousness; it is the truth if you are in Christ. You are a saint! If you begin to believe this truth, things in your life will drastically change.

Let's go back to Ephesians again, but this time, look at Chapter 2. Years ago, verse 6 changed my life, but let's start with verse 4. We have already looked at the first three verses where we saw that we were sinners. Let's pick up there.

"But God, being rich in mercy, because of the great love with which he loved us, even when we were dead in our trespasses, made us alive together with Christ—by grace you have been saved—and raised us up with him and seated us with him in the heavenly places in Christ Jesus" (Ephesians 2:4–6).

There are so many great and powerful truths in these three verses. Previously, however, I missed the power of verse 6. Notice the phrases *"raised us up with him"* and then *"seated us with him."* These are both written in the past tense, which means they are already accomplished facts.

Do you know what that means? I am writing this in Knoxville, TN, and you are reading this wherever you are located; but spiritually we are in Heaven if we are in Christ. That is what Paul says. We are alive in Christ, and in Him, we are raised up and seated with Him...right now! Dr. Solomon would often say, *"We must learn to become in experience, who we already are in position*[10]*."* Another one of his famous sayings is, "You can hang up your hang-ups at the cross and live in heaven on your way to heaven because you are already there!" If we are in Heaven with

Chapter Five

Christ, then doesn't it make sense that He calls us saints? This doesn't mean we are perfect, and Paul writes, *"To me, though I am the very least of all the saints, this grace was given, to preach to the Gentiles the unsearchable riches of Christ"* (Ephesians 3:10).

If we are seated with Christ in Heaven, then passages like Colossians 3:1–2 make more sense as well.

"If then you have been raised with Christ, seek the things that are above, where Christ is, seated at the right hand of God. Set your minds on things that are above, not on things that are on earth."

If we are seated in the heavens spiritually, then let us set our minds on this truth. Setting our minds here on earth brings fear, anxiety, and unrest. None of these exist in Heaven, so let us think about heavenly things and live in this reality!

You may be thinking, how can this be true? How can I geographically be where I am and spiritually be in Heaven? It is the same reason Paul can say we are raised with Christ. Romans 6:4, *"We were buried therefore with him by baptism into death, in order that, just as Christ was raised from the dead by the glory of the Father, we too might walk in newness of life."* We teach at GFI that in Christ we have been crucified, buried, and resurrected with Christ. This is a main theme of Paul's writings. How is it true? In Christ, we have received eternal life. I must confess that for years I thought eternal life began when I died. I would listen to John 3:16 saying, *"For God so loved the world, that he gave His only Son, that whoever believes in him should not perish but have eternal life."*

Then, I began to study and understand Paul's teachings. Eternal life isn't a thing but a person named Jesus Christ. Read with me John 17:3: *"And this is eternal life, that they know you, the only true God, and Jesus Christ whom you have sent."* What about 1 John 5:20, *"And we know that the Son of God has come and has given us understanding, so that we may know him who is true; and we are in him who is true, in his Son Jesus Christ. He is the true God and eternal life."*? Jesus is eternal life and when we receive salvation, we are given eternal life because we received Jesus. Eternal life, as you know, doesn't have chronological limits. Eternity isn't just future-focused; eternal life goes forward and backward. Psalm 90:2 confirms this: *"Before the mountains were brought forth, or ever you had formed the earth and the world, from everlasting to everlasting you are God."* Our life, that is, yours and mine as believers, has been placed into eternity. This means that because we have eternal life, we get a new future and a new past. How? We were crucified, buried, and resurrected with Christ. Our eternal life also makes it possible for us to already be in Heaven with Him.

You are not a sinner! Yes, you *still* sin, and that sin describes your life at that moment. But you are not a sinner; you are a saint! It is how Christ sees you!

---

[9] https://www.usccb.org/offices/public-affairs/saints

[10] *Handbook to Happiness,* Dr. Charles Solomon.

CHAPTER SIX

I remember growing up hearing how blessed we are to live in America. I didn't know what that meant until I began traveling to other parts of the world. When you walk around Haiti, Kenya, Ethiopia, Nicaragua, or Guatemala, you begin to see what people are talking about. However, when I speak to the people living in those places, I think maybe they also are the blessed ones. Let's go back to Ephesians 1, and I want to give you another true biblical identity statement about you. You are blessed!

"Blessed be the God and Father of our Lord Jesus Christ, who has blessed us in Christ with every spiritual blessing in the heavenly places (Ephesians 1:3)."

When I say, "You are blessed," I am not talking about the prosperity gospel. The Greek word for "blessing" means "to speak well of." Shara Drimalla writes in her Bible Project article, *What Does the Bible Say About Blessing?*, "The word 'blessing' brings to mind a variety of images for all of us. We say, 'Bless you!' after a sneeze or 'so blessed' when life is good, and we tag Instagram photos of a recent vacation with #blessed. Blessed is a religious-sounding word that we use a lot. But what does blessing mean? In the Bible, blessing refers to flourishing and the multiplication of life."[11]

The *Baker's Evangelical Dictionary of Biblical Theology* defines blessing as "God's intention and desire to bless humanity is a central focus of his covenant relationships. For this reason, the concept of blessing pervades the biblical record. Two distinct ideas are present. First, a blessing was a public declaration of a favored status with God. Second, the blessing endowed power for prosperity and success. In all cases, the blessing served as a guide and motivation to pursue a course of life within the blessing."[12]

Not too long ago, I was counseling a man, and he asked me something I had not previously thought of. He said, "Mark, the word *blessed*, or *blessing* is mentioned three times in this verse. That must be important, right?" Yes, our God is blessed, and he shares these blessings with all His children.

Do you know what this means for you and me? If we are blessed with every spiritual blessing, then we lack nothing. Years ago, while pastoring at Chilhowee Hills Baptist Church in Knoxville, TN, I was preaching through Psalm 23. Week one was Psalm 23:1, *"The Lord is my shepherd; I shall not want."* Here is what I told my congregation, "You lack nothing! You have everything you need in Christ." If the Lord is your shepherd, then you have everything you need. Notice I used the word "need," not "want." Of course, there are many things we may *want,* but in Christ, we have everything we *need* to do everything God has called us to do.

Chapter Six

Weeks later, before preaching one Sunday, I made this statement to a friend, "If only I had more grace, I would be a better pastor." My friend responded, "You have all the grace you need in Christ." Of course, I gave him a look because preachers do not like being preached to. Why did I think that? But worse, why did I believe it? You have heard it said that beliefs determine actions. What we believe will eventually affect our behavior and actions. This faulty view of lacking grace made me think I needed something more to be all God called me to be.

A lot of us make this false claim, stating things like, "If I had this or that, then I would be better." "If only I had patience, then I would be a better parent." Have you ever said that or at least thought about it? "If I had more grace, I would be a better boss." You see, if we believe we are lacking something, then we will use that as an excuse not to be who we really are!

Look at what Paul writes in Colossians 2:10: *"and you are complete in Him, who is the head of all principality and power"* (NKJV). Think about this for a moment. Please do not blow past this verse and keep reading. You are complete in Christ! Isn't that amazing? Paul explains this more in Colossians 2:11-12:

"In Him also you were circumcised with a circumcision made without hands, by putting off the body of flesh, by the circumcision of Christ, having been buried with Him in baptism, in which you were also raised with Him through faith in the powerful working of God, who raised him from the dead."

Not only are you not deficient, but you also have everything you need in Christ. While you are thinking about this, may I ask another question? What must you do to become more complete? The answer is nothing! If you are complete in Christ, then there is nothing left for you to do to make yourself more complete! What a relief, right?

While we are here, look at the verse before: *"For in Him dwells all the fullness of the Godhead bodily* (Colossians 2:9 NKJV)." If you wonder how we can be complete in Christ, then this verse is important to read and to believe. The fullness of the Godhead is in Christ, and we are in Christ, so the fullness of the Godhead is in us also. Paul starts this letter in chapter one to the church in Colossae, and he writes in verse 27, *"To them God chose to make known how great among the Gentiles are the riches of the glory of this mystery, which is Christ in you, the hope of glory"* (Colossians 1:27).

It is a mystery to me why many churches do not preach the biblical theology of Holy Spirit. May I explain why I think this? In Acts 9, you can read about Paul's conversion to Christianity. Before, he is called Saul of Tarsus, and on his way to Damascus, a light from heaven blinded him, and the voice of the Lord says, *"Saul, Saul, why are you persecuting me"* (Acts 9:8)? If you are new to this story, it is important to note that Saul was persecuting Christians. He was on his way to arrest believers after he approved Stephen's (another believer) execution via stoning, as we read in Acts 7.

Back to Acts 9. This encounter on the road changed Saul! It changed him so much that his name was changed from "Saul" to "Paul."

Chapter Six

"For some days he was with the disciples at Damascus. And immediately he proclaimed Jesus in the synagogues, saying, 'He is the Son of God.' And all who heard him were amazed and said, 'Is not this the man who made havoc in Jerusalem of those who called upon this name? And has he not come here for this purpose to bring them bound before the chief priests?' But Saul increased all the more in strength, and confounded the Jews who lived in Damascus by proving that Jesus was the Christ" (Acts 9:19b–21).

In the first chapter of Galatians, Paul states again,

"For I would have you know, brothers, that the gospel that was preached by me is not man's gospel. For I did not receive it from any man, nor was I taught it, but I received it through a revelation of Jesus Christ" (Galatians 1:11–12).

Paul continues by stating how he had *"persecuted the church of God, and he was advancing in Judaism, being extremely zealous for the traditions of the early fathers"* (Galatians 1:14–15). Then in verses 16b–18, Paul writes,

"I did not immediately consult with anyone; nor did I go up to Jerusalem to those who were apostles before me, but I went away into Arabia, and returned again to Damascus. Then after three years I went up to Jerusalem to visit Cephas (Peter) *and remained with him for fifteen days."*

Scholars have different opinions on what Paul did while he was there, but I believe it is safe to say that Paul's teacher was the Holy Spirit. Why is that important? Paul came back to preach, travel, and write a large part of the

New Testament. Paul uses a phrase a lot in his teaching. The phrase is "in Christ." The C.S. Lewis Institute, quoting John R.W. Stott, states, "The expressions 'in Christ,' 'in the Lord,' and 'in him' occur 164 times in the letters of Paul alone, and are indispensable to an understanding of the New Testament."[13]

We are blessed with every spiritual blessing *in Christ*! That is so important to know, trust, and understand. It would be great if Jesus were just *with* us, but how much more to know He is *in* us! Everywhere we go, there He is!

This is also the fulfillment of what Jesus told the disciples in both John 14 and 16. Jesus and the disciples were in the upper room before Jesus was arrested, falsely tried, and crucified. Scholars call this the "Upper Room Discourse." In John 14:16–17, Jesus said to the disciples,

"And I will ask the Father, and he will give you another Helper, to be with you forever, even the Spirit of truth, whom the world cannot receive, because it neither sees him nor knows him. You know him, for he dwells with you and will be in you." Jesus continues in John 16:7, *"Nevertheless, I tell you the truth: it is to your advantage that I go away, for if I do not go away, the Helper will not come to you. But if I go, I will send him to you."*

There are two things I want to point out in these verses. First, Jesus calls Holy Spirit the "Helper." Why? Jesus knew we needed help! Some other translations call Holy Spirit the Encourager or Counselor. I think all three are correct. In fact, let's be honest; most days I need help, encouragement, and a counselor! I think you will agree there are several, if not many, New Testament passages that are very difficult to obey. May I be honest with you? There are some that I do not want to obey. May I give you one verse that is hard for me? *"But I say to you who hear, love your enemies, do good to those who hate you, bless those who curse you, pray for those who abuse you* (Luke 6:27)." Is that easy for you? I do not want to be good to those who hate me. I want to ignore them or sometimes get even. Those who curse me, I often want to "bless them back," but not the way Jesus instructs here. I would tend to prefer the calling-for-justice type of Old Testament prayer instead of this radical love and mercy response. Therefore, praying for those who would abuse me would probably fit in better in the Old Testament prayers, but where is grace and love? So how do I obey? Through the Helper who is in me!

Second, Jesus said it is to our advantage that he goes away. Haven't you thought how great it would be to sit down to coffee with Jesus? I would ask questions and just sit and learn. But if he were with me at the coffee shop, then he would not be with you. What's the advantage? Holy Spirit is not with some of us but in all of us who are born again! It is so important for us to understand that Holy Spirit, the Lord God, is in us.

There is another reason why it is important to know that our identity is blessed. The flesh and our enemy within often make us wonder why God is withholding from us. I used to question why it seemed that some people had grace, while others, like me, lacked it. A lot of people think that if they read their Bible and pray, then God is happy with them. We never actually say that, but a lot of us live this way. The truth is that you lack nothing in Christ!

This is true of all in Christ, but it will not be true in you experientially until you actually believe it!

Having everything you need in Christ is the truth, but you must learn how to appropriate this. This is where discipleship comes in. It is so important to study Scripture, gather with like-minded people, and attend a church that preaches the fullness of the gospel. Knowing what I am telling you is the first step, but now you must trust it, and that comes through discipleship. We are saved by grace, and we continue to grow through sanctification by the same grace that saved us.

You are blessed! It is who you are. You lack nothing in Christ.

---

[11] https://bibleproject.com/articles/how-does-the-bible-explain-suffering/#:~:text=We%20say%20"Bless%20you!",and%20the%20multiplication%20of%20life.

[12] https://www.biblestudytools.com/dictionary/blessing/

[13] 'In Christ': The meaning and implications of the gospel of Jesus Christ by John R.W. Stott on June 3, 2007. Taken from https://www.cslewisinstitute.org/resources/in-christ-the-meaning-and-implications-of-the-gospel-of-jesus-christ/

CHAPTER SEVEN

Growing up, we always found a field or a court to play on. I was blessed to live in an area where other guys around my age loved to be outside and play sports. Here is how most days played out: two guys would be named "captains." The captains would be chosen depending on the sport, whether baseball, football, or basketball. Let's say we were playing basketball. Greg and Eric were chosen to be captains because, in our eyes, they were the two best players. We chose them to be captains because we did not want them on the same team together. That would be a great disadvantage to everyone playing on the other team! Everyone else would gather around for the first choice. You see, if you were chosen first, then everyone knew that either Greg or Eric thought you were the best!

Now if you were not chosen first, then the next victory would be not to be chosen last! Yeah, you guessed it, if you were chosen last then everyone knew you were the worst one on the court or the field! I had varying degrees of confidence based on each sport. For instance, in baseball, I would sometimes be chosen to be captain. When we played football, I knew I would not be chosen last. However, in basketball, I never knew how it would go down!

I remember one time going to a different part of the city to another field with a group of people I didn't know. I was there with one person I will keep nameless. We decided to play football, and as we threw the ball around, I thought surely someone would choose me. The captains were chosen, and the teams began to form quickly. Then it came down to me and the person I arrived with. I secretly hoped I would get chosen before him but what happened next completely threw me off guard. The captain said, "You can have the last two guys!" Not only did he not choose me, but he thought his team would be better with one less guy! He would rather play one man down than have me on his team!

Do you sometimes think that about God? I have a suspicion that a lot of people are living and falsely believing that God "puts up with me." We think, "God didn't want me, but He settled for me because He had to." Where does that come from? It is not in the Bible! Paul says that our identity is *chosen*. *"Even as he chose us in him before the foundation of the world, that we should be holy and blameless before him (Ephesians 1:4)."* This verse brings up different thoughts and emotions amongst believers. Some choose to argue the difference between God's sovereignty and man's responsibility. My goal is not to start an argument but to see how this verse speaks to our identity.

So, what does that mean? You, my friend, are a #1 draft pick. As I have mentioned, I was a baseball player, and I always had the dream to be chosen to play Major League Baseball. I graduated from college in 1998, and my dream would have been for the New York Mets to draft me in

Chapter Seven

the MLB draft that year. I imagined walking up on stage after hearing my name called, putting on a Mets jersey and hat, and fulfilling my dream of pitching for the Mets. That didn't happen, but I received something more powerful!

Paul isn't saying you were picked in the last round but first. He chose you first! For those of you who are not into sports, imagine that guy/girl you had a crush on, and they walked into school choosing you over everyone else! No matter what illustration you use, the fact is you are chosen, and notice, this has nothing to do with you. God doesn't choose based on performance like we did when we were kids. God chose us before the foundations of the world. This means before you did anything good to think you deserved to be chosen, or before you did something to think you were discredited or disqualified, God chose you. God chose you before you performed!

There is a small number of self-righteous people who think they are God's gift to this world. I doubt any of those people are reading this book. However, I think some of you reading this think you do not deserve to be chosen. Why? Is it because you haven't read the Bible enough? Let me ask you, "How much is enough?" Reading the Bible is very important but not for identity. We read the Bible because it is the Word of God and is one of the ways God communicates to us to teach us who He is and therefore who we are. We live in and by grace, and Paul writes, *"For Christ is the end of the law for righteousness to everyone who believes"* (Romans 10:4).

Do you not *feel* chosen because you had a bad past? Is this not why Jesus came? He came to save us and to give us a new identity! Listen to this truth found in 2 Corinthians 5:17–21:

"Therefore, if anyone is in Christ, he is a new creation. The old has passed away; behold, the new has come. All this is from God, who through Christ reconciled us to himself and gave us the ministry of reconciliation; that is, in Christ God was reconciling the world to himself, not counting their trespasses against them, and entrusting to us the message of reconciliation. Therefore, we are ambassadors for Christ, God making his appeal through us. We implore you on behalf of Christ, to be reconciled to God. For our sake, he made him to be sin who knew no sin so that in him we might become the righteousness of God."

You may feel like a loser, but you are an ambassador.

"But you are a chosen race, a royal priesthood, a holy nation, a people for His own possession, that you may proclaim the excellencies of Him who called you out of darkness and into His marvelous light" (1 Peter 2:9).

We do not find our identity in what we *do*. Our identity is found in what Christ has already accomplished on the cross. Remember the South African ministry to the street guys I mentioned in chapter four? As I walked them through their identity, as it is defined by God, I came to this verse about being chosen. I was praying while speaking and asking God how to relate this to these men. Then he showed me that rugby is a huge sport in South Africa. At

Chapter Seven

this time, it was a few months before the start of the 2024 Rugby World Cup. I asked the guys how many of them played rugby and most of them raised their hands. So, I had them imagine we were all players, and the coach was about to announce the first player chosen for the South African Springboks Rugby team. One of the guys looked like a rugby player; we will call him Steven. I built it up big, and then I announced the number one player chosen. The room filled with excitement, and then I yelled, "STEVEN!!!!"

For a second, I think we all forgot it was an illustration, as the man next to Steven gave him a high-five! I gave a second to allow everyone to settle down then I said, "This is what Christ did for all of you! He chose you first before you ever stole, broke the law, or even got saved and came to this ministry." Later that night, before we went to bed, Dr. John Woodward and I got a text from the ministry stating that the guys walked around the rest of the day telling everyone they were a #1 draft pick to God!

Do you believe this? You should, because it is true. God chose you! He loves you! You are His!

CHAPTER EIGHT

I love adoption! I love it for many reasons. One of my favorite reasons is that my youngest son is adopted from Ethiopia. I also have two nephews and a niece who were adopted from Ethiopia. Adoption is a huge part of our family, and through the passion of our family, many friends have adopted kids also. Did you know that you are adopted? This is another part of our identity. In Ephesians 1:5, Paul continues speaking about this identity we have in Christ when he writes, *"In love, he predestined us for adoption to himself as sons through Jesus Christ, according to the purpose of his will."*

It was God's plan to adopt us into His family. This is how we transitioned from orphans to become children of God. Imagine with me that you are in a courtroom. The judge is God, and you stand before Him convicted and condemned. In fact, you *know* that you are guilty. However, you have placed your faith in Christ alone to be your Savior, Lord, and Life. Right about the time you fear the gavel will fall and the decision given, Jesus says, "Objection, your Honor!" The enemy continues to accuse and throw out accusations, but Jesus continues, "Your Honor, these accusations are truthful. This person is a sinner, but I have paid for every sin they committed! Because they

Chapter Eight

placed their faith in me, they are no longer an enemy but my friend." God slams down the gavel and declares, "Not guilty!" Your ledger doesn't say condemned but justified!

That is a picture of the gospel of justification, and if that is all that happened, that would be amazing. *"Therefore, since we have been justified by faith, we have peace with God through our Lord Jesus Christ"* (Romans 5:1). But there is more, much more. Next, God says to you, "I see you are orphaned with no family. Not only do I declare you justified, but I also now adopt you as my child." How amazing! You walked into the courtroom alone and guilty, but you leave new, cleansed, and the Judge is now your father!

When we were in the adoption process with our son, my wife and I read a lot of books on adoption. We also studied adoption, especially as it is mentioned in the Bible. Adoption, as I mentioned, is a picture of the gospel. In adoption, the adopted son had all the rights and privileges of a son in the family. It is important to note that an adopted son did not become a slave but a son. Paul speaks to this fact in Galatians 4:4–7:

"But when the fullness of time had come, God sent forth his Son, born of woman, born under the law, to redeem those who were under the law, so that we might receive adoption as sons. And because you are sons, God has sent the Spirit of his Son into our hearts, crying, 'Abba! Father!' So, you are no longer a slave, but a son, and if a son, then an heir through God."

One truth we learned during our wait to adopt applies here. In Roman times, if I owed you money and could not repay it, then you could take me as a slave to repay my debt. You could also take one of my sons as payment as well. However, an adopted son was secure, meaning they were released from all previous debts. Suzie Klein wrote an article, "Adopted as Sons," and she states, "In the ancient world, the purpose of adoption was to preserve the family by providing an heir. The Greek word "huiothesia", which Paul used, means to "place as a son". Under Jewish law, there was no provision for adoption. When a man died without a son to continue his family line, his closest male relative was to marry the widow and produce an heir (the law of levirate marriage). So, Paul's term adoption as sons is not a reflection of Jewish law but a metaphor reflecting Roman law that allowed a man to provide an heir from outside his family. An adopted son was released from any debts or previous obligations and, as an heir, received all the rights, privileges, and responsibilities of sonship. In Romans 8:14–17, Paul wrote that as God's adopted sons, we become His heirs (see also Ephesians 1:11, 14). If we are His children, then we are heirs—*heirs of God and co-heirs with Christ* (Romans 8:17). Furthermore, according to Roman law, a naturally born baby could be disowned from the family. But an adopted child was chosen as a family member and, according to law, could not be disowned. He was a *permanent member* of the family. As believers, we are God's heirs and will never lose that privilege.

Klein continues with Paul's term "adoption as sons," which reflects another wonderful truth. At first glance,

Chapter Eight

you may think he is leaving women out or slighting them when he doesn't write "children" or "sons and daughters", but that is not the case at all. In his letters to the churches, Paul always includes all believers, both men and women. In Galatians 3:28, he wrote, *"there is neither Jew nor Greek, there is neither slave nor free man, there is neither male nor female; for you are all one in Christ Jesus."* There is no partiality with God. When God adopts us into His family, we all receive the rights of sons. This is important because in the Roman world, although female citizens had certain limited rights, they were far less than those of a man. Girls were rarely adopted because they did not provide a political advantage, nor could the family line be carried on through them. But when we are adopted into God's family, we all are given equal rights! We all have the rights of sons!"[14]

Part of our identity as adopted children of God is that we are totally secure in Christ. Back in Chapter 3, I quoted Colossians 3:3-4, which states, *"For you have died, and your life is hidden with Christ in God. When Christ who is your life appears, then you also will appear with him in glory."* This speaks to our assurance and security as believers. I do not wish to enter into a theological debate, but I do want to say that we cannot lose our salvation. The life we receive in Christ is eternal, not temporal. We did not earn our salvation, and therefore, we cannot lose it. Ephesians 2:8-9 reminds us that our salvation is not based on works but is received by grace through faith in Christ. Our salvation comes through the finished work of Jesus on the cross. Nothing more!

If our life is hidden with Christ in God, then who or what can break through God, Jesus, and Holy Spirit to take you away from Him? Read the end of Romans 8 and you will see the answer is "nothing or no one!"

"For I am sure that neither death nor life, nor angels nor rulers, nor things present not things to come, nor powers, nor height nor depth, nor anything else in all creation, will be able to separate us from the love of God in Christ Jesus our Lord" (Romans 8:38–39).

In Christ, we have both assurance *and* security. Assurance is all about today, but security speaks to all the tomorrows ahead. Not only am I safe in Christ today, but the Bible states that I will never get kicked out of the family of God. Remember that I am kept by the same grace that saved me!

What does Paul say in Colossians 3:4? *"When Christ who is your life appears…,"* who is coming with Him? You are if you are in Christ! How can you come with Him in the future, if you can be left behind? Your security of being with Christ and in Him at His second coming is not based on our works but on God's grace. The fact is we are in Christ and He is in us! When we are born again, we are adopted into the family as sons and daughters of the King! Our assurance and security don't come through our work. Some might argue, "Paul says we are to work out our salvation."

Yes, in Philippians 2:12, Paul writes

Chapter Eight

"Therefore, my beloved, as you have always obeyed, so now, not only as in my presence but much more in my absence, work out your own salvation with fear and trembling."

Paul doesn't say that we work *for* our salvation. He says we are to work it *out*. We are to work out what He is working in us. The salvation Paul is speaking of here is not justification. Theologically, justification is when you and I are declared right before God; it is when we are *born again* and *saved*. You can remember this by associating justification with the phrase "just if I'd never sinned."

"And you, who were dead in your trespasses and the uncircumcision of your flesh, God made alive together with Him, having forgiven us all our trespasses, by canceling the record of debt that stood against us with its legal demands. This He set aside, nailing it to the cross" (Colossians 2:13–14).

In justification, we are saved from the penalty of sin, which is why we must trust in Christ alone and His finished work on the cross.

What Paul is talking about here in Philippians chapter 2 is sanctification. In sanctification, we are being (*currently*) saved from the *power* of sin. Again, the same grace that justifies us sanctifies us. We are not saved by *grace* and kept by *works*. Just as we are saved by grace through faith, so we are sanctified by grace through faith. However, faith works; it produces fruit, and it works absolutely. As we believe and trust God in life, it is right in line with what Holy Spirit is working to teach us, and it produces the fruit of the Spirit through us. When we are saved, we are not just to sit around and do whatever we want. No, we are called to be salt and light to the world! Jesus Himself said in the Sermon on the Mount,

"You are the salt of the earth, but if salt has lost its taste, how shall its saltiness be restored? It is no longer good for anything except to be thrown out and trampled under people's feet. You are the light of the world. A city set on a hill cannot be hidden. Nor do people light a lamp and put it under a basket, but on a stand, and it gives light to all in the house. In the same way, let your light shine before others, so that they may see your good works and give glory to your Father who is in heaven" (Matthew 5:13–16).

How do we work out our salvation? By participating and cooperating with Christ through the obedience of faith. It's more than just following the example of Christ; it is allowing the power of Christ to flow through us into further obedience. To work out means "to use, to exercise it." Now, because Holy Spirit dwells within us, we are blessed with every spiritual blessing (Eph. 1:3). We lack nothing, and Holy Spirit is working within us to exemplify and express the life of Christ in us and out through us, producing the fruit of the Spirit: joy, peace, love, long-suffering, gentleness, and self-control (Galatians 5:22–23)! The issue is not that we lack something that we must work hard to get but that we do not often make withdrawals! Let me explain this principle. In the world economy, when we take out of our accounts, we have less. For example, if

Chapter Eight

I go to an ATM to withdraw cash and spend that cash to purchase an item, the withdrawn amount is subtracted from my account. My account then is less than it was before the amount was taken. This is true because there are even items in your mind right now that you want, but there are not enough funds in your account to purchase the item you want. You cannot take out more than what is in the account!

This is not true in Christ. In Christ, we can take out continually, and our spiritual account remains full. How is that possible? You and I have received the fullness of Christ. We received *all* of the Holy Spirit; no more is coming, because He didn't leave any out. But there is more; in Christ, we all have the same amount of the Spirit. I think many have the false belief that the pastor of the church we attend has the most amount of Holy Spirit. Then maybe the other pastors, elders, deacons, and church leaders have less but then there are those sitting in the pew, and we have the least amount. Not true! We all have the same amount, and that amount is the fullness of Christ in us.

But let us also ponder this...God does not run dry! You can continually make withdrawals, and your account will never be in a deficit. How does this look practically? Let's say you have a boss or manager who is hard to work for. How do you pray for your day? Do you just ask God to bless the day or maybe help you to make it through with a boss that's difficult? Not bad prayers, but what if we prayed more specifically? What if we asked Holy Spirit for longsuffering, gentleness, joy, and patience to live victoriously in the midst of dealing with a difficult boss? Now we are making withdrawals from the unlimited resources we have in Christ. Living victoriously amid difficulty then is not just praying but also making these withdrawals in Christ. We are working out what He has put in...we need to be using all we have in Christ!

Notice, Paul says in Philippians 2 to do this with *fear and trembling*. We are not to be terrified of God but *in awe*, which means "a holy respect and an attitude of worship and admiration." Let's look at the next verse because it is a game-changer. Philippians 2:13, "*For it is God who works in you, both to will and to work for his good pleasure.*" We can *work out* our salvation because God is at *work within us*. You are not called to do all this alone in your own power! Jesus speaks to this plainly in John 15:5 when He says, "*I am the vine; you are the branches. Whoever abides in me and I in Him, he it is that bears much fruit, for apart from me you can do nothing.*" How much can you do without God? Nothing, zilch, nada! The problem is we try to, *daily*!

Our adoption is so important because we are no longer orphans but children of God. How amazing to believe that we walked out of the courtroom with God no longer as our Judge but now as our Father! Please do not hear the truth "Children of God" and just breeze on by. How amazing to know we are His children, and He is our Father. I remember as a kid being around other children bragging about what our fathers did. One may say, "My dad is a manager," and another say, "My dad owns his own company!" As a child of God, I can say, "My Father created your dad; He created everything."

Chapter Eight

There is another powerful truth here in our adoption. My friend recently told me, "I have only gone to ask for forgiveness from God as my judge once. But I go to him daily for forgiveness, as my father." Because I am a child of God, I do not go into a courtroom but into the living room. Recently, I had to go into a courtroom, and even though I was not the one on trial, I was nervous. The judge had on his robes, and the environment was not kind or friendly. However, the situation would be different if the judge took off his robe, laid down the gavel, and invited me for coffee. In Christ, He is not my Judge; He is my Father!

---

[14] https://www.disciplersonline.org/blog/adopted-as-sons

CHAPTER NINE

"I have accepted Christ, but I am not sure he has accepted me." I cannot tell you how many times I have heard that line or one like it. It is a statement based on *works*, not *grace*. We just saw that the working out of our salvation is exercising the faith we have in Christ. We are working *out* what He has worked *in*. The person who thinks they haven't been accepted by God has prayed a prayer or at least has some form of religion, but they are not sure they have done enough to earn the affection, love, and acceptance of God. Paul caps off our truths of identity in Ephesians 1:6, *"to the praise of the glory of His grace, by which He made us accepted in the Beloved* (NKJV)."

Do not read this verse and skip the significance. He, that is Jesus, *made* us *accepted*! We do not *make* ourselves *acceptable*. We have all tried to make ourselves acceptable, failed miserably, and then felt unacceptable! This is why we try so hard to be *right* with God based on our *checklist* of Christianity. We have falsely believed that reading the Bible, praying, giving, attending church, evangelizing, and much more makes us *acceptable* to God. These things are good things, but being accepted is the *work* of Jesus, and it is a *work* of grace. Again, notice Paul starts this verse by stating, *"To the praise of the glory of His grace."* We do not

Chapter Nine

deserve to be accepted, but Jesus has chosen to declare it so! You and I being accepted, again, doesn't come from our work or even from our potential to be good later in life. It comes from Jesus, not from anything else!

Paul finishes verse six with, "...*in the Beloved.*" Beloved is capitalized by the translators, because Paul is showing us that the Beloved is Christ. When you see the name "Beloved," what do you think about first? Think about this for a minute. For me, I think about Jesus' baptism. Jesus came from Galilee to John the Baptist at the River Jordan. Jesus came to be baptized, and at first, John denied being worthy to baptize Jesus. When he gives in and baptizes Jesus, Matthew writes,

"And when Jesus was baptized, immediately he went up from the water and behold, the heavens were opened to him, and he saw the Spirit of God descending like a dove and coming to rest on him; and behold, a voice from heaven said, 'This is my beloved Son, with whom I am well pleased" (Matthew 3:16–17).

Charles Haddon Spurgeon, speaking of this verse in 1862, wrote, "A thousand sermons would never exhaust the theme of the union of the Church with Christ. No doctrine is sound that does not recognize this, and no experience can be very profound which does not lead the soul more clearly and more fully to rejoice in this most glorious truth. Probably it is a doctrine more suitable to advanced Christians than to young believers; but where the Lord enables the heart to feed upon it, it will be found to be food at once nourishing, delicious, satisfying, and strengthening."[15]

God called Jesus "Beloved." Why? You are likely thinking the reason is He healed people, fed 5,000 people, and raised people from the dead. Yes, He did those things and more, but all of that happened after God said He was *pleased* with Jesus. God knew what He would do! You are right; He knew, but He said it, not from potential, but in truth! He says the same thing about you!

You are accepted because of *who* Jesus is. We are accepted in Christ, and like everything we have stated, the key to all of this is *in Christ*. He saved you, and He keeps you, and it is all by grace that comes from your union with Christ. Paul writes in Colossians 1:9–12,

"And so, from the day we heard, we have not ceased to pray for you, asking that you may be filled with the knowledge of his will in all spiritual wisdom and understanding, so as to walk in a manner worthy of the Lord, fully pleasing to him: bearing fruit in every good work and increasing in the knowledge of God; being strengthened with all power, according to his glorious might, for all endurance and patience with joy; giving thanks to the Father, who qualified you to share in the inheritance of the saints in light."

Do not miss the truth contained in verse 12, *"giving thanks to the Father, who qualified you to share in the inheritance of the saints in light."* Who *qualifies* you? It is not you but the Father. Again, these truths are true because we are *in Christ*! When we know and believe who we are in Christ, it is easier to know what to do. How is it easier? I say it is easier for two reasons. First, we know that we are

Chapter Nine

in Christ, and He is our power. He is the fuel that makes it easier. But there is another reason: we know the *outcome* doesn't change our *standing*. No matter what happens, I am still a saint, blessed, chosen, adopted, and accepted.

Being accepted is so important to both believe and understand. Why? Acceptance is the way out of rejection. Let me conclude the same way I started. I will ask you once again, "Who do you think you are?" You are a saint! You are blessed, which means you lack nothing. You have all you need in Christ. You are chosen! God chose you before the foundations of the earth, that is, before you did anything good or bad. You are adopted, which means you are secure. And finally, you are accepted!

Do me a favor, or better yet, do yourself a favor. Stop listening to the negativity all around you! Instead, listen to Jesus! Jesus said, *"If you abide in my word, you are truly my disciples, and you will know the truth, and the truth will set you free" (John 8:31–32).* When you are free, then there are no obstacles that can hold you back. Being free leads to victory.

I have always believed one main reason for negativity is to keep us from doing what God has called us to do or to keep us stagnant at best. Some people reading this book have struggled because they do not *believe* these identity truths. Why? Some have never been taught this from the pulpit. But others, unfortunately, have been told hurtful things in their life. Believing these statements has made them into what they are today.

At Grace Fellowship International, we call this "rejection." Dr. Charles Solomon wrote a book called, *"The Ins and Out of Rejection."* In the book, he defines

Who Do You Think You Are?

rejection as the lack of meaningful love.[16] He doesn't mean that there was no love in an individual's life but that for whatever reason, the love wasn't meaningful nor edifying. Notice the title of the book again. The "ins" is plural, because Dr. Solomon states that there are many ways for us to be rejected. Some rejection is overt, or obvious. These might include:

- Abuse of any kind.
- Statements like, "I do not love you anymore." "I wish you had never been born."
- Ill-treatment from a parent or stepparent.
- Being forced into adult responsibilities before adulthood.
- Being given up for adoption.

However, some rejection is covert and not obvious. These would include:

- The premature death of a parent or sibling.
- Broken home and absentee parents.
- Favoritism of a sibling.
- Overprotective parents.
- Being "seen but not heard."

What happens when we are rejected? Not everyone is the same but here are some emotional reactions to rejection:[17]
- Feelings of worthlessness.
- Wishing you had not been born.
- Feelings of inferiority.

Chapter Nine

- Inability to express feelings.
- Depression.
- Emotional insulation.
- Subjectivity, introspection, or perfectionism.
- Worries, doubts, and fears.
- Self-condemnation, self-hatred, and guilt.

Many times, when I am counseling or coaching someone struggling due to rejection, I show them this list and I ask them, "Which of these do you identify with." Do you see what I did there? You see, every one of us has dealt with rejection. Some may be more or worse than others, but we have all been rejected, and we have all rejected others. Be honest with me; how many of you relate more to this list of emotional reactions to rejection than to the identity statements of Ephesians 1:1–6?

When negativity strikes, when we mess up, and when things go wrong, we feel worthless and inferior. We even say things like, "I am such a mess up; I cannot do anything right." If we mess up badly, we think, "It would be better for everyone if I had never been born!" Others, however, never show or express any feelings because they were never allowed to as children.

I keep reaffirming your identity in Christ because I want you to *believe* it and *trust* it *daily*. You are not what you feel! Remember, *"fact over emotion."* In John 8:32, Jesus didn't say we are set free by how we *feel*. We are set free by the *truth*! So, what's true? It is not our feelings, because our feelings change based on our circumstances.

The truth is Jesus, and I have tried throughout this book to point you to Him, the truth!

Can I point out one more thing about the title "Ins and Out of Rejection." I have shown you the "Ins," but the word "Out" is singular. Why? There may be many ways to be rejected, but there is only one way out, and that is through acceptance. Yes, I may have been rejected by my family, friends, or co-workers, but I overcame it through the truth of Ephesians 1:6, which said that we are *"accepted in the Beloved."* True biblical identity, when embraced by us through faith, changes us!

Consider this: have you accepted your acceptance? I hear Dr. Woodward ask people this almost on a daily basis. It is not just that you have accepted Him, but He accepts you, and He makes you acceptable because of who He is and what He has finished. As a child, maybe in summertime, did you ever come to the dinner table dirty? Your mother probably said, "Go get cleaned up and make yourself presentable!" Some of you may be fighting this urge currently. You feel like you need to get "cleaned up" so you can become acceptable. Here is the good news: in Christ, you are already both accepted and acceptable.

---

[15] https://www.spurgeon.org/resource-library/sermons/accepted-in-the-beloved/#flipbook/

[16] *Ins and Out of Rejection*, by Dr. Charles Solomon.

[17] Taken from Grace Fellowship International "Finding Joy" seminar notebook.

CHAPTER TEN

The change that comes from knowing your identity *in Christ* starts now! A big question in the world we live in today is, "What do you identify as?" The world has all kinds of responses. Maybe you have used some of them. How have those worked for you? You are *not* worthless. I know some of you may *feel* inferior, but you are *complete* in Christ; again, read Colossians 2:10. You may have *wished* you had never been born, but Jesus *chose* you before the foundations of the world; read Ephesians 1:4. Maybe you have struggled with self-condemnation and self-hatred, but the truth is you are a saint; read Ephesians 1:1. There are a number of glorious declarations that God makes about you that directly confront and contradict the lies that the enemy (the world, the flesh, and the devil) may cause you to hear or feel through various rejections in life.

Let me close with a word that changed my life. The word was so powerful that I had it tattooed on my side so I would see it every morning as I got ready. The word is "*reckon*." "Wait, what?" Surely you are not serious. I am serious, and don't call me Shirley! (Sorry, one of my wife's favorite movies is *"Airplane.*[18]*)* I live in the South, and many times you hear the word "*reckon*" being used as a guess. I will give you an example. "Mark, what are you doing after work today?" "I reckon I will head home and eat dinner with the family." However, the word "reckon" in this case is not a calculated guess. The word means "to calculate the cost." In Greek it is an accounting term, and it has the idea of counting something to be personally true of you.

It is easy to just say, "This is true of you, Mark, because you wrote the book." Nope! It is true of me because I am in Christ. It is also true of you if you have been born again in Christ. However, it will not be true in your experiences until you reckon (trust) it to be so.

Let me give you an example of what reckoning means. To my younger readers, do you remember checks? I know I am dating myself. We used to carry checkbooks instead of cash. For us to pay a bill, a check user would write a check, which meant putting an amount on a piece of paper, writing to whom the check would be payable, signing the bottom of the check, and adding the date before giving the check to the person or company we owed a debt. Now let's say I need $100. I see you, ask you for money, and you write me a check for $100. When do I receive the money? A check is not like cash. If you give me a $100 bill, then the money is immediately mine when I have it in my possession. A check is different. For the money to be mine, I must sign the back of the check and take it to the bank. Only then will the $100 be credited to my account.

You and I must reckon these truths to be true because they are true! These five identity statements of Ephesians 1 are like a check in your pocket. They are true, but they will not change your experiences unless you endorse the check. You must sign the check and take it to the bank! Reckon

Chapter Ten

these truths to be so. You are a saint who is blessed, chosen, adopted, and accepted in the Beloved! This will change your life, and it will change how you live out everyday life. These statements are true of you currently, but they won't become true in you until you believe them.

Reckoning is different than knowing something. Knowledge is what I know in my mind. It is intellectual. Knowledge, however, does not always lead to transformation. Transformation happens when what I know in my mind becomes the truth I live by because I begin to trust it! Do you remember being a kid and doing trust falls? One person would stand in front of another. The person in the back would raise their arms tightly in front and the person in the front would place their arms out like forming a "T." Then the person in front would fall back and hopefully land safely in the arms of the person standing behind.

In 4th grade, we had to do this for a participation grade, and there was a boy in my class who would always allow people to fall. When the teacher said to pair up, everyone must have moved at the speed of sound, and there I was left with that boy, the one who allowed everyone to fall. I remember thinking, "I am not going to do this", but the teacher made me. He promised to not allow me to fall. He lied. I fell and everyone laughed. But that boy in my 4th grade class is not like Jesus. You may not be able to trust people in a "trust fall," but you can trust Jesus. He will not allow you to fall. He will catch you every single time!

"Now to Him who is able to keep you from stumbling and to present you blameless before the presence of his glory with

great joy, to the only God, our Savior, through Jesus Christ our Lord, be glory, majesty, dominion, and authority, before all time and now and forever. Amen" (Jude 1:24).

The enemy and your flesh have lied to you, saying, "The Lord has allowed you to fall over and over again." No, friends, He just allowed you to fall lower than you wanted. Your heart is beating, and you wonder why, but Jesus never allowed you to hit the ground, even though you *felt* like He did. He has never failed you or let you down. You feel farther and longer than you wanted, but He still caught you!

There is a victorious life available to you every day in every situation. It starts when you know who Christ is and then who you are! So, let me ask you again, who do you think you are? If your sense of identity has been based on your past, your emotions, or your performance, I challenge you to exchange this old identity, which doesn't work, for a new, secure, grace-based identity in Christ.[19]

---

[18] "Airplane" July 2nd 1980, by Paramount Pictures.

[19] To receive counseling and/or coaching from Mark, please email Mark@gracefellowshipinternational.com

PUBLISHER'S APPENDIX

<u>What is Exchanged Life?</u>

The heart of our message is our union with Christ in His death, burial, resurrection, and ascension. This is often referred to as the exchanged life. At the moment of our salvation, God took us out of spiritual death in Adam (Romans 5:12-21) and "transformingly" put us into union with Christ (Romans 6:1-10). Christ exchanged our old identity as sinners in Adam for a radically new identity in Christ (2 Corinthians 5:17). We are now not just sinners saved by grace; our essential nature and identity is that of new creation saints in Christ (Ephesians 1:1). Our union with Christ is so real, so vital, so complete, so trans-historical that the old us (our spirit) in Adam died and was buried. The new us (our spiritual identity) is now raised up in union with Christ. We have been set free to live as ones who have been recreated in Christ's resurrection (Romans 6:11). This is all God's doing. He traded our old spiritual identity in Adam for a new spiritual identity in Christ.

This is the foundation of the exchanged life: God's uniting us with Christ, whose life is eternal, victorious, and abundant. This results in a shared life, a life of union with

Christ. However, the usual experience for us as Christians seems to be that we lose sight of our resources in Christ. The great tendency is for us to try to get our needs met our own way and depend upon our human resources (the flesh) instead of trusting Christ. Even the Apostle Paul described his own personal struggle and defeat as he strived in his own strength to fulfill the will of God (Romans 7:14–25).

As we continue to appropriate by faith His life rather than relying on ourselves, Christ meets our inner needs and gives us His joy, peace, power, and a deeper walk with Him in the midst of life's difficulties and problems. The focus of our attention is shifted from ourselves to Christ and those He has put into our lives for Him to love through us (John 15:9–17; 1 Corinthians 13; Galatians 5:13–18; 1 John 3:16–4:12). This is the result of the exchanged life. By an ongoing trust in Christ as our life, we can trade our total insufficiency to live the life the New Testament describes for Christ's total sufficiency to live it in and through us. If you don't like your life, exchange it for a new one[20]!

---

[20] https://gracefellowshipinternational.com/about-gfi/what-is-exchanged-life/

Grace Fellowship International

Many times, our ministry gets confused for a church, and with our name, I can understand why. Grace Fellowship International (GFI) is a counseling, coaching, and chaplaincy ministry built around what men like Watchman Nee and Hudson Taylor called the "Exchanged Life." Our vision at GFI is to "Guide people into a complete and victorious identity in Christ."

We use the word "complete" because we desire for people to be healthy spiritually, emotionally, and physically. Our goal is not to help just in some areas, but in *all* areas of life. We use the word "victory" as Jesus states in John 10:10 that He came "that they may have life and have it abundantly." We not only believe the verse, but we also believe believers can live abundantly daily. I have never met anyone who didn't desire victory. However, how many of us have been taught the victorious way?

Since 1970, Grace Fellowship International has helped members of the body of Christ to experience, mature in, and communicate effectively the message of identification with Christ in His death, burial, resurrection, and ascension in their various spheres of influence, so that all may know Christ as Savior, Lord, and Life.

During this time, we have helped countless people live victoriously while also dealing with anxiety, depression, addiction, fears, and other emotional issues. Victory is not the absence of difficult circumstances. Victory is Christ, and He is in us so we can live victoriously while dealing with all the difficulties of life.

Our Exchanged Life counseling is free! For over 50 years, we have counseled while only asking for donations. In counseling, we cover issues of rejection, and identity, discuss what the Bible calls "flesh," and how to exchange a life that doesn't work for one that does! To get more information on our counseling methodology, schedule an assessment, or learn how to become certified with GFI, please visit www.GraceFellowshipInternational.com/counseling/

What is Life Coaching?

Life Coaches help people maximize their lives for success today and for all the tomorrows coming! Coaches honor the client as the expert in his or her life and work and believe every client is creative, resourceful, and whole (spiritually, emotionally, and physically). Standing on this foundation, the coach's responsibility is to empower and encourage clients. At GFI, we desire to improve the client's outlook on work, life, and their spiritual journey while improving and unlocking their true identity in Jesus Christ. We motivate our clients to strengthen their spiritual core, to be firmly planted, connected in Christ, and rooted in God's Word.

"As you therefore have received Christ Jesus the Lord, so walk in Him, rooted and built up in Him and established in the faith, as you have been taught, abounding in it with thanksgiving" (Colossians 2:6-7).

When you realize and believe in your identification with Christ, that you were crucified, buried, and raised with Christ, your life will be healthier, stronger, and victorious!

Grace Fellowship International Coaching

GFI offers coaching to individuals, pastors, leaders, businesses, ministries, churches, and influencers. Our Life Coach Guides are all certified Life Coaches and have obtained an Exchanged Life certification through GFI. Our coaching focuses on exchanged life principles, walking in the Spirit, and the importance of trust and surrender to Christ. The coaching relationship is the vehicle of change and transformation.

Is Coaching for Me?

Self-care is important to your soul care. Your growth and transformed life matter. What would it look like for you to stop striving in this life and start thriving? We are not designed to be driven by our emotions but to be set free by the truth of God (John 8:32). Our coaches are trustworthy, communicative, and motivating. You can expect that our coaches are joyful, empathetic listeners, will ask curious questions, and are concise communicators. Our coaches coach people and not problems.

Comparing Counseling with Coaching

- Both provide relationship improvement and overall wellness.
- Counseling deals with the past while coaching is future-oriented and proactive.
- Counseling is more problem-focused and coaching is more solution-focused.
- Counseling works toward emotions while coaching works toward outcomes.
- Counseling gives recommendations but coaching does not give advice.
- Coaching is about growth, not healing. Coaches walk alongside clients, not in front of them[21].

Director of Coaching Ministry

Mark McKeehan

Memberships:

American Association of Christian Counselors
International Christian Coaching Association.
Light University:

- Professional Life Coach
- Health and Wellness Coaching

ISSA:

- Personal Training
- Fitness Coach
- Elite Trainer
- Specialist in Strength and Conditioning

Schedule a Coaching Meeting

To learn more about our coaching methods or to schedule a coaching session, please:
- Call GFI at (865) 429-0450
- Email <u>coaching@gracefellowshipinternational.com</u>

---

[21] Some of this information is taken from the AACC Light University Coaching curriculum.

WHAT HAPPENED TO ME?

Romans 5:1 – I have been justified (completely forgiven and made righteous).

Romans 6:1-6 – I died with Christ and to the power of sin's rule on my life.

Romans 8:1 – I am freed forever from condemnation since I am in Christ.

1 Cor. 1:30 – I have been put into Christ by God's doing.

1 Cor. 2:12 – I have received the Spirit of God into my life that I might know the things freely given to me by God.

1 Cor. 2:16 – I have been given the mind of Christ.

1 Cor. 6:19-20 – I have been bought with a price. I am not my own. I belong to God.

2 Cor. 1:21; Ephesians 1:13-14 – I have been established, anointed, and sealed by God in Christ and have been given the Holy Spirit as a pledge (a deposit/down payment) guaranteeing my inheritance to come.

2 Cor. 5:14-15 – Since I have died, I no longer live for myself, but for Him (Christ).

2 Cor. 5:21 – I have been made righteous in Christ.

Galatians 2:20 – I have been crucified with Christ and it is no longer I who live, but Christ lives in me. (The life I am now living is Christ's life.)

Ephesians 1:3 – I have been blessed with every spiritual blessing in heavenly places.

Ephesians 1:4 – I have been chosen in Christ before the foundation of the world to be holy and without blame before Him.

Ephesians 1:5 – I was predestined (determined by God) to be adopted as a son/daughter.

Ephesians 1:7-8 – I have been redeemed, forgiven, and am a recipient of His lavish grace.

Ephesians 2:5 – I have been made alive together with Christ.

Ephesians 2:6 – I have been raised up and seated with Christ in Heaven.

Ephesians 2:18 – I have direct access to God through the Spirit.

Ephesians 3:12 – I may approach God with boldness, freedom, and confidence.

Colossians 1:13 – I have been delivered (rescued) from the domain of darkness (Satan's rule) and transferred to the Kingdom of Christ.

Colossians 1:14 – I have been redeemed and forgiven of all my sins (the debt against me has been canceled). See Col. 2:13,14.

Colossians 1:27 – Christ Himself is in me.

Colossians 2:7 – I have been firmly rooted in Christ and am now being built up in Him.

Colossians 2:10 – I have been made complete in Christ.

Colossians 2:11 – I have been spiritually circumcised (my old, unregenerate nature has been removed).

Colossians 2:12-13 – I have been buried, raised, and made alive with Christ.

Colossians 3:1-4 – I died with Christ, and I have been raised up with Christ. My life is now hidden with Christ in God. Christ is now my life.

2 Timothy 1:7 – I have been given a spirit of power, love, and self-discipline.

2 Tim. 1:9; Titus 3:5 – I have been saved and called (set apart) according to God's doing.

Hebrews 2:11 – Because I am sanctified and am one with the Sanctifier (Christ), He is not ashamed to call me brother/sister.

Hebrews 4:16 – I have the right to come boldly before the throne of God (the throne of grace) to find mercy and grace in times of need.

2 Peter 1:4 – I have been given exceedingly great and precious promises by God by which I am a partaker of the divine nature (God's nature).[22]

---

[22] Taken from GFI's "Finding Peace" Seminar Notebook and used with permission.

JESUS CHRIST THE LORD HAS BECOME MY LIFE (Philippians 1:21, Colossians 3:4)

THUS HE IS

My Strength	Psalm 27:1
My Wisdom	1 Corinthians 1:30
My Sanctification	1 Corinthains 1:30
My Righteousness	2 Corinthians 5:21
My Redemption	1 Corinthians 1:30
My Peace	John 16:33; Ephesians 2:14
My Victory	1 Corinthians 15:57; Colossians 2:15
My Joy	John 15:11
My Hope	Colossians 1:27
My Obedience	Hebrews 10:7
My Spiritual Fullness	Colossians 2:9,10
My Goodness	Galatians 5:22
My Source of Love	John 17:26; 1 John 4:8
My Kindness	Galatians 5:22
My Source of Forgiveness	Luke 23:3-4
My Patience	Galatians 5:22
My Rest	Matthew 11:28; Hebrews 4:10
My Self Control	Galatians 5:25
My Freedom	Colossians 2:16,17

Who Do You Think You Are?

My Gentleness	Galatians 5:25
My Spiritual Mind	1 Corinthians 2:16
My Faithfulness	Galatians 5:22
My Access to God	John 14:6; Ephesians 2:18

WHO AM I?

1. GOD

I am His Creation – made in His image (Gen. 1:26,27)
I am His Child. He's my loving Heavenly Father (1 John 3:1)
I am an individual. A one-of-a-kind handmade original with a God-given personality (Ephesians 2:10)
I'm me. I'm precious in His sight. (Psalm 116:15)

2. JESUS CHRIST

I'm His, for He bought me with a price – His life (1 Corinthians 6:18-20)
I'm accepted in Him (Ephesians 1:6)
He loves me without reservation or qualification, with an everlasting love (John 3:16; 1 John 3:1; Psalm 52:8, Jeremiah 31:3)

3. THE HOLY SPIRIT

I'm indwelt by Him (John 14:17)
I'm regenerated by Him (Titus 3:5)
I'm sealed by Him (Ephesians 1:13,14)

I'm made safe and secure under God's ownership (John 10:27,28)

4. MY FAMILY

I'm _____ (husband/wife/child) responsible to respond and provide that which God's Word commands me to do (in love).
I'm _____ (dad/mother/son/daughter) and enjoying a godly relationship with them.

5. GOD'S FAMILY

I'm a member of the Greatest Family in heaven and on earth! Joined to every other member of the Body of Christ, locally and worldwide. Enjoying the privilege of fellowship with many of God's own.

6. OTHER PEOPLE AT WORK/PLAY

I'm relating to a great bunch of choice folks in a loving church fellowship. Enjoying wonderful fellowship with fellow workers (at church) and developing sharing relationships with friends, relatives, and work associates (witnessing as a goal).

7. IN TIME...

I'm a person under construction – in process, not a finished product, but growing in the grace and knowledge of our Lord and Savior Jesus Christ. Possessor of eternal, abundant life in Christ. Joint heir with Christ of all that's His. Everything that belongs to Jesus belongs to me for I am in Him and He is in me.

8. IN ETERNITY

I'll receive the fullness of my inheritance: a resurrection body, knowing as I am known, glorified, experiencing the glorious liberty of the sons of God, conformed to the image of God's Son.

www.ingramcontent.com/pod-product-compliance
Lightning Source LLC
Chambersburg PA
CBHW070623050426
42450CB00011B/3110